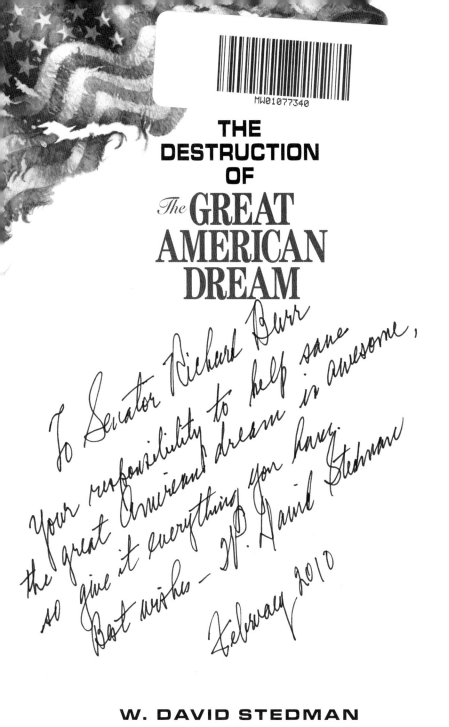

# THE DESTRUCTION OF
## *The* GREAT AMERICAN DREAM

*To Senator Richard Burr*

*Your responsibility to help save the great American dream is awesome, so give it everything you have.*

*Best wishes — W. David Stedman*

*February 2010*

## W. DAVID STEDMAN

THE DESTRUCTION OF THE GREAT AMERICAN DREAM

© Copyright 2009 by W. David Stedman

First Edition, 2009

Published By
W. David Stedman

Produced By David Collins

Distributed By Sedgefield Graphics, Inc.
5313 High Point Road
Greensboro, North Carolina 27407

Printed and Bound in the United States of America

The Destruction of the Great American Dream

Stedman, W. David

ISBN 978-1-61658-580-8

foundersprinciples.com

# TRUTH

*When will we Americans have the courage to face the TRUTH? The truth is that we are in the process of destroying the beautiful American dream...truly the great hope of the world.*

*Many years of concern, and now agony and sleepless nights, have pushed me to write this book. We must not fail to rise to the challenge of our lifetime...to do EVERYTHING we can to save the country we love and spare our children and grandchildren the pain from our selfish, national indulgencies.*

George Washington
Father of our Country
**First President of the United States**

# Remember

## *"We the People"*

It is ultimately
OUR responsibility
to guide this nation

*GIVE a man a fish, feed him for a day.*

*TEACH a man to fish, feed him for a lifetime.*

*Lao Tzu*
*Between 4th and 6th Centuries, B.C.*

## *a note from the author*

This is not a Republican book, nor a Democratic book. It is a book for true-blooded, patriotic Americans. It is a plain, straightforward statement on the forging of the greatest nation on earth, how and why it was created, the philosophical structure and principles that made it possible, and how and why it is now in great danger. There are powerful forces at work today which would change our free society to some form of statist, socialist government. My concerns for our country are greater now than ever before. My goal is to do everything in my power to help save the wonderful America we have known. It is my hope this book will encourage you to do the same.

# Dedication

To my wife, Sarah,

my eternal soulmate

# ACKNOWLEDGEMENTS

My deep appreciation to LaVaughn G. Lewis, Co-Editor with me of both *Our Ageless Constitution* and *Rediscovering the Ideas of Liberty*. Her work with constitutional scholars and her own intensive study of the Founders' writings have lead her to work hard to preserve their ideas of liberty. To Dr. George W. Carey, Professor of Government at Georgetown University, I am deeply indebted for his comments on American sovereignty and for his philosophical contribution of the Founders' views of human nature. My special thanks to my friend, Dr. Peter Greer, former Deputy Undersecretary of the U. S. Department of Education, for his frank and most helpful critiques. I am very grateful to my daughter, Dr. Nancy Jane Calloway, for her excellent insights and help with the manuscript. To my wife, Sarah, I can never thank her enough for her devoted support and work with all aspects of this book. Her constant encouragement has been a source of great inspiration. My appreciation to Richard Creed and Pattie Stoltz for their helpful comments. My gratitude also to my friend David Collins, the very insightful and talented producer of this book, who has gone to extra lengths to make it the best possible. And my thanks to Chris Gibson, a fine technician, for his help with the computer.

A special appreciation to Edward B. Hagy, Jr. for his outstanding artistry in the design of two of our former books: *Our Ageless Constitution* and *Rediscovering the Ideas of Liberty*, and now, *The Destruction of the Great American Dream*.

# THE DESTRUCTION OF *The* GREAT AMERICAN DREAM

## CONTENTS

# Chapter 1

# THE GREAT AMERICAN DREAM

Today we are witnessing the destruction of the great American dream. It is in deep trouble. This dream, which we have cherished for well over 200 years, is disappearing right before our eyes. Evidence of this trouble is accumulating rapidly, but even without this evidence, we somehow sense it and know it.

This is not only the dream of Americans, but of countless millions of people around the world, most of whom will never get to America to experience it. We are still the most fortunate people on earth to have LIVED the dream. Yet we know things are not right now with our beloved America.

Our nation was born in freedom and protected by our Constitution, but the constitutional principles have been much abused through the years. Now we see large corporations taken over by government and labor unions. We see great financial institutions brought under the control of government. We see the power of central government expanding to an alarming degree and creating incredible and unsustainable debt. We are astonished that our President has stated boldly on several occasions that our Constitution is a "flawed document."

America is at a major crossroads in its history, the most serious since the Civil War. Our country seems headed toward some sort of statist, socialist government. If that should happen, the Great American Dream will surely be destroyed. We must not allow that to happen, for it will take with it the heart and soul of America.

Remember, Americans are different. We are different in our heritage of freedom, different in our spirit of industry and achievement, different in our concern for the human rights of people around the world, and different in our outreach to the future. Our great strength among all nations lies in these DIFFERENCES, not in our conformity to THEIR ways. But we are now being crush-molded into something distinctly European. Our Great American Dream is being smothered by the lust for power, the lust for wealth, and our complete failure to educate each generation of young Americans on the principles of government for a free people. These three unfortunate developments have paved the way for a movement toward the national centralization of our government, which has been going on slowly for many decades, but is now greatly accelerating. If this relentless drive toward centralization continues, it must eventually lead to tyranny.

To be in position for making the critical decisions to correct the course, we must first understand how this Great American Dream came to be, what it is exactly, and what is required to salvage and protect it. So let's go back to the beginning for this understanding.

We begin with the citizens of the original thirteen British Colonies in the 1770s. They had become incensed and deeply resentful of the oppressive taxation, regulation, and controls of the British Parliament, and of King George III in particular. After all, they were more than three thousand miles away at a time when the fastest means of communication was by horseback and sailboat. Great controversy was brewing, and it culminated in the Colonists declaring on July 4, 1776, in a written Declaration of Independence, that they were free and independent from British rule. Then followed five years of difficult war with England until finally, with the help of the French military, American freedom was secured by the defeat of the British at Yorktown in 1781.

After this great victory, major developments began to take place in the new America. That same year, the Articles of Confederation, originally drawn up in 1777, became effective when ratified by the thirteenth state, Maryland. While the Articles were a noble effort at unification and cooperation, they were too weak to hold the states together. These problems were addressed by the Constitutional Convention held in Philadelphia in 1787. The delegates to this convention were authorized to meet only for the purpose of revising the Articles of Confederation. Instead, much to their surprise, and dismay of some, a great miracle occurred in Philadelphia when the Convention swept away the Articles as such, creating an entirely new document: the Constitution of the United States.

This new Constitution was such a different and startling concept that it quickly attracted attention around the world. For the first time, all authority was recognized as coming from our Creator, who endowed all people with certain inalienable rights. The people, in turn, gave to government only that power the people wanted it to have. Let us emphasize that these God-given rights of the people were now to be protected by the very limited authority and power that the people themselves had delegated to government. The Founders' idea was that the principal functions of government were to protect the inalienable rights of the people and to protect the people from violence and fraud. In their minds, the smaller the government, the better— at last, "We the People" lived in maximum freedom.

The selling of the new Constitution to the people and to the legislatures of the various states was accomplished primarily through the Federalist Papers. These were written individually by James Madison, Alexander Hamilton and John Jay. Altogether 85 Papers were published. Each of these presented cogent reasoning why a particular aspect or provision of the new Constitution was appropriate and necessary. The Federalist Papers were so well written Thomas Jefferson commented that they constituted "...the best commentary on the principles of government which has ever been written."[1] Even so, it took a while for ratification to be completed.

Although the ratification by the thirteenth state, Rhode Island, did not occur until 1790, the course for the nation had already been set. It was truly a new day. In the years that followed, many fortunes were made and dreams realized by the people who lived in the colonies. As word spread around the globe, other people began to realize what coming to America could mean to them and their families.

People dreamed of living in America where they could know personal freedom in a truly democratic society that offered them almost unlimited opportunity. No restrictive legislation. No government breathing down their necks. Freedom to practice their religion in their own way. Incredible opportunities for advancement. All one had to do was set sights high and then work hard to achieve the goals. One could start with practically no money and eventually become the owner of a business enterprise, an owner of a farm or the holder of a good job. In many cases, the government gave 160 acres of farmland to homesteaders under the Homestead Act of 1862. All of these opportunities were possible. Many had turned possibility into reality. For the first time in their lives, people had the chance to utilize their abilities and realize their ambitions to the fullest extent.

The Census Bureau estimates the total population of the Colonies in 1790 was almost 4,000,000. By 1820 it had doubled, by 1850 it had doubled again, and by 1880, 1920, and 1980, it had doubled three more times.[2] More immigrants have come to America than to any other nation, and they have made an inestimable contribution to the success and stature of our country.

This early phenomenal immigration was composed primarily of people from England, Scotland, Ireland, Holland, France and Germany. These immigrants were characteristically good, hard-working people. Later many came from the Scandinavian countries, and much later others arrived from eastern and southern Europe. In the last several years, all past waves of immigration have been eclipsed by an illegal " invasion" of some fifteen million illegals pouring across our southern borders. Some people continue to seek the legal route and wait for years to come to America, while others board overcrowded boats just to get the chance to swim ashore where they would at last be safely a part of this nation and the American Dream.

Just what was it that made The Great American Dream possible? No other country in the world offered anything like this. It was a peculiarly American phenomenon. Rousseau had said earlier that "…Man is born free, yet he is everywhere in chains." [3]

But not in America, for at last, the Americans were free. Free to do as they would, free to go their own way, and they went in a direction no others had gone, starting with a totally different concept of government for a free people. With the new freedom came the birth of The Great American Dream. The free exchange of goods and services was a natural outflow of their newly found liberties. Free markets lead to what came to be called a free enterprise economic system with an entrepreneurial spirit, which were, in reality, simply CAPITALISM. Conceptually, capitalism is just that simple—a natural outflow from an environment of freedom. People seem to forget that elementary fact. **Capitalism is perhaps the greatest evidence of a free society**.

The philosophical foundation, in conjunction with the Founders' Principles, represented a major departure from the past and a magnificent achievement by a most gifted and unusual group of leaders. The signers of the Declaration of Independence and the Constitution included men of great intellect and character, university educated in many cases and intimately knowledgeable about the political works of Aristotle, Solon, Cicero, Locke, Montesquieu and others. They were also well aware of the political systems of the Greeks, Romans, and especially, the English. It was an extraordinary group of talented people—names like Madison, Jefferson, Adams, Washington, Hamilton, Franklin, Hancock, Morris, Mason, and Henry. Their government was constructed on enduring concepts and principles that deal with the very nature of man. This put a flavor of the eternal to what they had created, somewhat like the eternal concepts expressed as The Ten Commandments.

As a consequence of their newfound freedom, the original thirteen British Colonies became the greatest among all nations over the next 150 years. It was an absolutely phenomenal feat. The Chinese had been unable to do anything like this in some 10,000 years, the Egyptians in 7,000 years, or the Greeks in 5,000 years. The Colonists had found the secret of unleashing the collective power of individuals who now were reaching out to achieve to the best of their abilities. This environment of freedom and achievement encouraged great development in practically all areas---industrial, social, educational, scientific and religious. In the meantime, the boundaries of America pushed from the Atlantic to the Pacific. America had become the greatest industrial and military power in the world and was producing three times more Nobel Prize winners than Germany, the next country in line.

Today America stands as the only superpower in the world. Yet the real superpower of America is not to be found in its industry, nor in the size of its army or navy, nor in the striking force of its fighter jets and bombers, nor even in its stockpile of nuclear bombs. The great power and influence of America is the compelling spirit and passion of The Great American Dream, whose protection is the philosophical foundation and the Founders' Principles of government for a free people.

# Chapter 2

## The Philosophical Foundation and the Founders' Principles
### of Our
## Government for a Free People

Essential to an understanding of the uniqueness, the power, and the influence of America is an understanding of its philosophical foundation and the Founders' Principles that were built on this foundation. Both the philosophy and principles can be gleaned from the Declaration of Independence, the United States Constitution, the Federalist Papers, and the writings of the Founders.

In our republic, the people hold the sovereign power. If the sovereign American people do not understand the philosophical foundations and the principles of liberty and their responsibility to protect them, they will not be able to preserve over time the greatness of America and the freedom of its people.

While there have been some experiments with citizens' rule throughout history (notably Israel, under Moses, the Athenian City States, and the Roman republics), for the most part, people have been ruled and controlled by government, whether by a tribal chief, a feudal lord, a king, or an emperor. The people were allowed only the limited freedom their government was willing to give them. This same relationship has persisted in modern times in such forms as dictatorships and politburos. This condition can be shown graphically as follows:

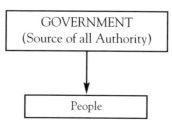

As the graph indicates, most of the power is in the government. This government-citizen relationship is referred to as Rulers' Law.

There was always the tendency of those in power to abuse it. The people had not yet learned, or were unable, to control such abuse.

This condition underwent a major change in 1776, when the American colonies revolted against the tyranny of English rule. The American Revolution was as much a culmination of a revolution of political thought as it was a war of revolt. The Declaration of Independence was the first formally adopted political document that provided a radically new philosophical foundation for a free society. This new approach may be diagrammed as follows:

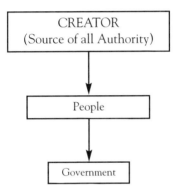

As early as the first century B.C., Cicero had written that supreme law comes from God, but this concept had never before been formulated in any national public declaration. In this concept, the people recognized that all primary rights ("unalienable rights") are derived directly from our Creator. The Founders' plan was to set up a structure of government to protect those rights. Since the unalienable rights were understood to belong to the people, the people would grant to government only those rights and powers they were willing for government to have. Thus government became the servant of the people. All government was now to be administered through laws made by the people themselves. This is an example of the Rule of Law in contrast to the centuries old Rulers' Law.

Although this philosophy of rights and power became the cornerstone of our new form of government, there was another philosophical dimension which needed to be built into the structure of government to make it successful. After all, the government at all levels must be administered by officials who are drawn from the ranks of the electorate. They must be given the power to carry out the responsibilities assigned to them. But these officials are human beings and bring to their office all the weaknesses of human nature. The Founders were well aware of the historical political record of countless examples of the failure of leaders and officials of government resulting from greed, treachery, threats, terror, dishonesty, and even the actual killing of people who got in the way. Thomas Jefferson went straight to the point when he said "…In questions of power then let no more be heard of confidence in man but bind him down from mischief by the chains of the Constitution." [4] And bind them down they did. (See an excellent essay on The Founding Fathers' View of Human Nature..., by Professor George W. Carey of Georgetown University, Our Ageless Constitution, pages xxvi-xxvii).

The Founders first separated the principal powers of government into the three branches of executive, legislative and judicial, and then built in many so-called "checks and balances." For instance, legislation is passed by the vote of each house of Congress (one a check on the other), then consolidated before being sent to the President for signing. The President approves or vetoes. Congress can override his veto by a 2/3 majority vote. This structure was indeed a stroke of genius and served our nation well for a long time. Today, however, we may be facing a serious test of this as a result of our many abuses of our Constitution

Having identified the source of all authority as their Creator, and having addressed in the structure of the Constitution the way to deal with the troublesome parts of human nature, our founders had established the philosophical foundations of government for a free people.

The signers of the Declaration of Independence, and later the framers of the Constitution in 1787, are not to be looked upon as originators of all the ideas and principles they adopted. They were, however, the synthesizers and activators of a long train of political thought. Nothing like this had ever been done before.

The Founders studied, sifted, and debated these great ideas of the past . Out of this process evolved a general acceptance of certain basic principles which we call the Founders' Principles (sometimes known as First Principles). Never before had these principles been synthesized as a basis for a new structure of government which provided for order and justice while protecting the liberty of the people.

Among the Founders' Principles were: *

1. Creator-Endowed unalienable rights of the people;

2. Purpose of government:
   To protect the unalienable rights of the people, and
   To protect the people from violence and fraud;

3. Natural law-ultimate source of constitutional law;

4. Rule of law, not of men;

5. Justice for all;

6. Innocent of any crime until proven guilty;

7. No cruel and unusual punishment;

8. A virtuous and moral people;

9. People educated to understand the principles of government for a free people;

10. Government as close to people as possible – limited federal government; strong local and state governments;

11. Separation of powers with checks and balances;

12. Constitutional limitations on government's power to tax and spend;

13. Economy in spending; prompt payment of public debt;

14. Money with intrinsic value and standards of weights and measures;

15. Strong defense capability;

16. Supremacy of civil over military authority;

17. Right of the people to keep and bear arms;

18. Decisions by the majority within a Constitutional framework;

19. Representative government with free and frequent elections;

20. Right to speedy trial by jury of peers;

21. Rights to ownership of private property and encouragement of commerce;

22. Freedom of religion;

23. Freedom of individual enterprise;

24. Freedom of speech and the press;

25. Freedom of person under the protection of habeas corpus;

26. Due process of law;

27. No ex post facto laws or bills of attainder;

28. No unreasonable searches and seizures;

29. Grand Jury indictment of capital crimes before a person may be held to account;

30. Peace, commerce, and honest friendship with all nations; en tangling alliances with none;

31. A written constitution – the supreme law of the land – prescrib ing within itself the only lawful methods of amendments by its keepers, the people;

32. No laws giving more favorable treatment for members of Congress than for the citizens.

A fact usually overlooked is that religion played a very important role in the development of our founding documents and the structure of our new government. The people who settled the American colonies brought with them from Europe institutions of civil government and systems of law which had been developed over centuries in environments strongly influenced by Judeo-Christian thought. The Declaration of Independence recognized a Supreme Being in four significant manifestations of sovereignty.

Professor M. E. Bradford's research has shown that at least 47 of the 56 signers of the Declaration of Independence were Christians and perhaps as many as 53 of the 55 men who participated in the Constitutional Convention were Christians. All through the colonial days, the pulpits of America were alive with discussion or promotion of some political principle, event or person.

The impact of this can be better understood when we consider the statement by Dr. Archie Jones, then Director of Research, Plymouth Rock Foundation: "Because religion is fundamental to ethics, people's religious view of the world and life is also fundamental to law and politics. To be sure, the political process determines what laws are to be enacted, but the ethical views of those who dominate the political process determine what commands they will enact as law."

America has become the envy of the world. What a unique and magnificent heritage has preceded us, and how very important it is for us to maintain it! But, how can we maintain it when we have become a nation of constitutional illiterates, ignorant of the philosophy and principles which protect our liberty? Justice Story, a distinguished member of the Supreme Court during the 19th century, wrote to the young people of America:

> "Let the American youth never forget that they possess a noble inheritance, bought by the toils, and sufferings and blood of their ancestors....It may, nevertheless, perish in an hour, by the folly, or corruption, or negligence of its only keepers, THE PEOPLE."[35]

The fragile nature of liberty is the compelling reason our schools must never fail to make instruction in the founding principles one of their most important and cherished commitments.

In following through on such a commitment, it is essential the students study the original documents so they can catch the brilliance and spirit of the founders.

* This list of Founders' Principles was first published in *Rediscovering the Ideas of Liberty,* Co-Editors, W. David Stedman and La Vaugn G. Lewis (Principle 32 was added later).It is not necessarily exhaustive, although it is intended to be as extensive as we could make it after our own investigation and consultation with others. Different scholars would perhaps state some of the principles differently, or perhaps add some, or go into greater detail in certain instances. We only submit this list as our best effort to describe the specific nature of the Founders' Principles. There is no order of priority in the list, and the numbers assigned to them have no meaning except to provide a quick and easy reference system. We know of only one other consolidated list of this nature.

# Chapter 3

## THE BEGINNING OF TROUBLE

Somewhere along the line bad things began to happen in America. It is impossible to put an exact date on the beginning of real trouble in the expansion of our government, some of which was actually unconstitutional. It is certain, however, that vital channels of free action in the marketplace began to choke up in the early part of the last century. Over time, this choking was bound to have an impact on the aspirations of individuals through tens of thousands of new, and sometimes complicated, laws, regulations, and restrictions. Incrementally, these laws and restrictions did not cause a big problem, but collectively, over the years, they became overwhelming. It reminds us of the story of the bullfrog in the pan of cold water. If the temperature is increased incrementally, the frog will allow himself to be cooked to death.

In the early days of the new republic, there had been little government interference in the marketplace. In 1890 Congress did pass the Sherman Antitrust Act to protect small business from the monopoly of large, powerful corporations. However, the largest concentration of these new developments began during the presidency of Franklin D. Roosevelt, and in the mold of preceeding Progressive Presidents Teddy Roosevelt and Woodrow Wilson. The central government created many new agencies and programs in an effort to combat the destructive force of the Great Depression of the early 1930s. This increasing bureaucracy and government control has continued to grow through the presidencies of both political parties. The cumulative choking effect may be bringing our nation dangerously close now to critical mass in terms of holding on to The Great American Dream.

An illustration of the massive growth of these new laws and bureaucratic regulations is the growth of the number of pages of the Federal Register required to print the regulations imposed on the marketplace. In 1936, 2,411 pages were required; in 1950, 9,562 pages; in 1960, 14,479 pages; and in 1978, 61,261 pages,[5] twenty-five times the number from four decades earlier. The Department of State reported that by the early 1990s there were over 100 federal regulatory agencies.[6] Apparently, in the minds of the politicians and bureaucrats, the American people had reached the point they needed these 100 agencies to tell them what they could and could not do. The real truth is that the politicians and bureaucrats need to understand that THEY WORK FOR US ... WE DO NOT WORK FOR THEM.

This pernicious growth of government has continued at a rapid pace until today. We are now sloshing around in a morass of laws, regulations and bureaucracies. Senator Lamar Alexander, R- TN, was quoted recently by George Will as saying, "There are at least 60 congressional committees and subcommittees authorized to hold hearings on auto companies and most of them will, probably many times."[7]

Our country turned a critical and worrisome corner in 1978 when the U. S. Chamber of Commerce reported there were more people receiving regular government checks than there were workers in the private sector.

We have now reached the tipping point where our legislation is so complicated that just one bill may consume as many as 1,800 or more pages--- so long that few Senators or Representatives of Congress ever read the entire bill before voting on it. This is an outrageous dereliction of duty and an insult to the people who elected them. James Madison made a comment on such a situation in saying, "...It will be of little avail to the people...if the laws be so voluminous that they cannot be read, or so incoherent that they cannot be understood...."[8] It is all further evidence of the destruction of the environment for The Great American Dream.

Another set of critical developments was also taking place during recent years. These developments directly involved the U. S. Constitution where great damage has been done by the so-called activist judges. They have no hesitation or fear in turning their backs on what the Framers meant when they wrote the Constitution, and they proceed to replace the original concepts with what they themselves think it ought to be. In this way, it has been possible for these judges to bypass the Constitution, thereby avoiding the lengthy and difficult process of amending it. As a consequence of these developments, our Constitution, as it was originally intended to be, has suffered much distortion, including substantive change.

Still, a third set of developments has been our abuse of the Founders' Principles through the years. We have gotten away from them by simply ignoring them or by bending, twisting, or legislating them to suit our immediate purpose. The consequence of this is, again, a further weakening of our system of a free society.

Fourth, there has been a vicious attack on religion in America, especially in more recent years. Religion has always been a very powerful force in this country since the very early immigrants came here to escape religious persecution in their own countries. In the Declaration of Independence, the Colonists referred to their belief in a Supreme Being in four ways as : Creator, Nature's God, Divine Providence, and Supreme Judge of the World. Religious freedom was so important to the citizens of early America that they insisted their religious freedom be spelled out more clearly than had been done in the original text of the Constitution, and thus it became an integral part of the First Amendment.

Finally, beginning with the establishment of the unconstititional Federal Reserve Bank in 1913, and especially in recent decades, our federal government has increasingly practiced reckless financial management. This ranged from pressing banks to make home loans to people who could not possibly repay them, to shameless, irresponsible spending, all of which undermined the already fragile financial structure of our nation

# Chapter 4

# The Destruction
## Of the
# Great American Dream

To understand the frightening erosion of our Constitution, our Founders' Principles, our freedom, and our capitalistic system, it is important to review some examples of these major changes which have occurred through the years. Keep in mind the remarkably prophetic warning of President Andrew Jackson on the occasion of his farewell address on March 4, 1837:

> "...You have no longer any cause to fear danger from abroad...It is from within, among yourselves, from cupidity, from corruption, from disappointed ambition, and **inordinate thirst for power**, that factions will be formed and liberty endangered. It is against such designs, whatever disguise the actors may assume, that you have especially to guard yourselves...." [9] *(emphasis added)*

## 1. Largest Debtor Nation

We are now the largest debtor nation in the world, whereas formerly we were the largest creditor nation. Our debts are so great that no one can possibly understand them, not even the astronomers who constantly work with incredible numbers. It is now reported that if we take our actual debt and add to it all the unfunded liabilities facing us, the total is well above 50 trillion dollars. This is most surely the pathway to national bankruptcy. We have already been warned that our nation may lose its AAA bond rating. Our greatest funder, the Chinese, seem to be very concerned about it, even if we are not.

America has been considered the LEADER of the world. What a shameful embarrassment for America.

Recommendation:

Congress must not spend in excess of income. If they refuse to do that, then the citizens must take a defiant position and vote them out of office. Do we really have the courage and the will to do this?

## 2. Monetary System

The Federal Reserve Bank is an unconstitutional organization performing the unconstitutional function of issuing our currency. The Constitution makes it clear in Article 1, Sections 8 and 10, that only Congress has the power to coin money and to regulate the value thereof. But Congress doesn't issue the money any longer. It is done by the Federal Reserve Bank, a private banking cartel whose books the Congress is not allowed to see, although it was Congress who created the Fed. Who is in charge here? Certainly not the Congress.

Recommendations:

a) Abolish the Federal Reserve System

b) Congress must reassume its constitutional responsibility for issuing the currency. Congress should conduct a complete audit of the Federal Reserve Bank (Congressman Ron Paul, a great patriot, is currently sponsoring a bill to audit the Fed via House Bill H.R. 1207 and Senate Bill S. 604.[10] Press your Senators and Congressional Representatives to support this important legislation).

## 3. Prompt Payment of Debt

Our Founding Fathers believed we should pay government debt promptly, as it was not the responsibility of subsequent generations to pay the debts of their fathers. But we never pay the public debt. It just gets larger every year, until most recently it has essentially spiraled out of control. How can future generations ever pay the public debt we have now created? Recent generations are without doubt the most selfish of all generations, because we want right now much more than we can pay for. We borrow ever more money to satisfy our perceived needs, but have no thought of paying for the things we are consuming. We just leave it to our children, grandchildren, and great grandchildren to pay for our squandering through a lower standard of living for themselves. We can enjoy OUR luxury by letting THEM pay for it. How very clever of us! How very cruel of us!

Listen to the contempt of the Founders regarding debt. Thomas Jefferson: "The principle of spending money to be paid by posterity under the name of funding is but swindling futurity on a large scale...."[11] James Madison: "I go on the principal that a public debt is a public curse."[12] Again to Thomas Jefferson: "...we must not let our rulers load us with perpetual debt. We must make our election between economy and liberty, or profusion and servitude".[13]

Recommendation:

Stop the squandering. We have dug a very deep hole for ourselves and our grandchildren. We must find a way to pay our debts and get on a current basis. We took decades to get into our financial mess, and it will take time to work out of it, but work out of it we must. Do we have the courage and the will to do this?

4. Money Without Intrinsic Value

The dollar referred to in the Constitution was the then current dollar which had been defined by the Articles of Confederation as so many grains of gold or silver. The delegates at Philadelphia were most fearful of a paper dollar and had voted in committee overwhelmingly against paper dollars. The Colonies had experienced a terrible period when their continental dollar had become almost worthless because of the lack of gold and silver backing. In fact, it was so bad that if something was essentially worthless, it was often referred to as "not worth a continental."

Our fiscal policy over the last several decades has been wildly irresponsible, and this responsibility lies directly at the doors of the Federal Reserve Bank and Congress. We have printed and borrowed money at a feverish rate, always going deeper into debt, and always pushing off the payment of this debt to our children and grandchildren. It is a downward spiral that must end soon or we will be facing national bankruptcy. We may be reaching the point where our dollar is "not worth a continental" all over again.

In 1933 Congress declared the dollar no longer redeemable in gold. In 1965 coinage of the constitutional silver dollar was terminated. The final blow came in 1968 when Congress declared the dollar no longer redeemable in silver. So the dollar is now only a piece of paper that the government declares is a dollar. It is "fiat," or funny money, and no nation's currency has ever survived a monetary system based on paper money. Fiat currency has always ended in disaster. On this subject, The Daily Reckoning reports, "...EVERY fiat currency since the Romans first began the practice in the first century has ended in devaluation and eventual collapse, of not only the currency, but **of the economy that housed the fiat currency as well**. (*emphasis added*.)" [14]

"Post-World War l Weimar Germany was one of the greatest periods of hyperinflation that ever existed...the sums of money to be paid by Germany were enormous, and the only way it could make payment was by running the printing press... Here is a brief timeline of the marks per one U. S. dollar exchange rate:

April 1919: 12 marks
November 1921: 263 marks
January 1923: 17,000 marks
August 1923: 4.621 million marks
October 1923: 25.26 billion marks
December 1923: 4.2 trillion marks"[15]

Is this to be our fate? We now talk in terms of trillions of dollars of debt, yet we trudge on, ignoring our Founders' Principles of government for a free people, thinking we can, in some mystical way, print all the paper money we want and the markets will continue to accept it. How dumb! How sad!

Recommendation:

A way must be found to provide once again intrinsic value to our currency in order to regain the faith and trust not only of Americans, but also of people around the world.

Associated with this subject is the fact that for many years the American dollar has been the reserve currency for the world. Due to such poor handling of our nation's fiscal affairs, other nations, notably China, are promoting the idea of replacing the reserve status of the American dollar with a basket of other currencies. If this should occur, it would be a financial catastrophe for the dollar and our country, for then we could no longer print paper money to pay our international debts but would have to earn it instead.

5. Constitutional Limitation on Federal Spending

Article I, Section 8 of the Constitution specifies exactly those expense items for which the Federal government is allowed to tax. (Take a few minutes and read Article l, Section 8 in the Constitution in the Appendix).This list of allowed expenses has been ignored by Congress and other leaders for many years, and now the Federal government taxes to spend money for whatever purpose it chooses. Because of our generation's greed and selfishness, we are spending money as if there is no tomorrow, without regard to the morality involved and the resulting punishment of future generations.

Both our President and Congress now, and for many years past, don't seem to understand the simple truth that the government must live within its income. Why can't they understand that? Most everybody else does. Their failure to abide by the constitutional limitations of Article 1, Section 8 has greatly accelerated the growth of a centralized, controlling government.

Andrew Jackson was hard on this principle. In his Farewell Address he said, "…there have always been those who wish to enlarge the powers of the General Government. There is but one safe rule…confine (it) within the sphere of its appropriate duties. It has no power to raise a revenue or impose taxes except for the purposes enumerated in the Constitution…Every attempt to exercise power beyond these limits should be promptly and firmly opposed." [16]

Recommendations:

a) Congress must live by the constitutional limitations on spending. If they don't, then we must vote the big spenders out of office. If we don't follow through on this, then WE are the problem. Do we really have the courage and the will to follow through?
b) Make the personal income tax a flat tax.
c) Eliminate the capital gains tax.
d) Eliminate taxes on dividends (double taxation).
e) Eliminate the death tax.
f) Cut corporate taxes significantly.

## 6. Private Property Rights

In 2005, In Kelo v. City of New London (CT),[17] the city had forcefully taken a parcel of land from a private owner and transferred it to another owner to be used as part of an economic development for the private gain of the new owners. The Supreme Court, in a 5-4 decision, approved. The fundamental right to private property has been a cornerstone in our society. John Adams expressed the Founders' view on private property in the strongest terms, "The moment the idea is admitted into society, that property is not as sacred as the laws of God, and that there is not a force of law and public justice to protect it, anarchy and tyranny commence."[18] Kelo v. City of New London is but an early step in demolishing one of our key inalienable rights as a free society.

Recommendation:

We must return to the supremacy of private property rights. A government has no right to take private property from a legitimate owner and transfer it to another for some financial gain.

## 7. States' Rights

The Tenth Amendment is the states' rights amendment. For many decades the federal government has enacted program after program which shift power away from the states to the central government.

This led retiring Supreme Court Justice Sandra Day O'Conner to say, "Congress will nibble away at state sovereignty, bit by bit, until some day essentially nothing is left but a gutted shell." [19] This practice is just the opposite of the Founders' intentions.

Recommendation:

The states must launch a study to determine what rights of theirs have been unjustifiably taken over by the federal government and then take action to reclaim those rights.

8. Government Takeover of Private Enterprise

In recent months we have seen the incredible action of the federal government taking control, either directly through actual ownership or through massive loans, of some of our largest industrial and financial enterprises. Madison, Washington and Jefferson must be looking down in utter horror at this devastating development. It is a major blow to the basic concepts of our capitalistic system and cannot be tolerated.

Recommendation:

All such government intervention must be stopped. Let the normal market forces deal with the problems.

9. A Living Constitution

In recent years much has been said about our "Living Constitution." These are code words for the work of the activist judges, which means we have a constitution that changes and evolves over time in accordance with the needs of the times as interpreted by those judges. It is a most insidious and dangerous development. Our judges are supposed to interpret the law as written, not create new law, as these judges sometimes do. They simply ignore the fact that the Constitution was written and signed as meaning just what was intended by those who voted on it. Alexander Hamilton must have foreseen the possibility of such shenanigans when he wrote, " Until the people have by some solemn and authoritative act annulled or changed the established form, it is binding upon themselves collectively, as well as individually; and no presumption, or even knowledge of their sentiments, can warrant their representatives (the executive, judiciary, or legislative) ; in a departure from it, prior to such an act."[20]

We do have a living constitution, but it is in an entirely different sense from that of the activist judges. It is living in the sense that we can constitutionally change it, but it can be done in only two ways, as provided in Article 5 of the Constitution. An ammendment may be proposed:

(a) By the vote of two thirds of both Houses of Congress to be ratified by three fourths of the States, or

(b) By the vote of two thirds of the States calling for a Constitutional Convention for proposing one or more ammendments to be ratified by three fourths of the States.

It is difficult to change the Constitution this way, but it was the intention of the Founders to make any change difficult. Even so, the Constitution has been changed many times . We now have 27 amendments.

We would never consider such a thing as the "Living Ten Commandments" in the sense of the current constitutionally activist judges, changing them as we would. Neither should Americans ever consider the idea of a "Living Constitution" in the activist sense.

Recommendation:

We must get rid of the activist judges and replace them with judges who interpret the constitution in light of what was intended by those who wrote it. Getting rid of federal judges will be difficult and take time. The President nominates them and the Senate confirms, so this means that We the People must put a President and Senate in place who understand the Founders' Principles.

10. Educating Citizens on Principles of Government For a Free People

**Possibly the greatist mistake America has made through the years has been its failure to teach each successive generation the philosophical foundations and the Founders' Principles of government for a free people.** Having this knowledge provides a measuring stick for judging the work of the judges, legislators and other politicians through the years and enables the electorate to measure how far off course they may be getting before it is too late. How can an electorate protect its form of government from unscrupulous political maneuvering if it does not understand what the philosophy and principles are? Of course, they cannot.Thomas Jefferson made it quite clear when he said, " I know no safe depository of the ultimate powers of the society but the people themselves: and if we think them not enlightened enough to exercise their control with a wholesome discretion, the remedy is not to take it from them, but to inform their discretion by education. This is the true corrective of abuses of constitutional power." [21]

For close to 100 years our educators, including the administrators, the Boards of Education, the teachers, and the unions have all failed to realize the absolute priority of giving our students a good understanding of the fundamentals of our form of government, both the philosophy and the Founders' Principles. Throughout the academic community there has been a notable lack of interest and resolve about teaching these fundamentals. We should never have arrived at this critical state in our nation that we are facing today. Is it possible there have been forces at work who *intended* to short circuit this particular component in educating our students? (Dumb the people down and you can lead them wherever you want them to go). When the understanding of the foundations and principles of America are withheld, power is transferred to government.

Recommendation:

Set up a required semester course on the philosophical foundation and Founders' Principles of government for a free people for both high school and college levels. Make a passing grade a requirement for graduation. The development of such a course is now in the works. In the appendix you will find recommended legislation to accomplish this for public schools. Work at the local level to create a strong demand for this semester course.

There are some 16,000,000 high school students in America today. Of these, it is estimated that approximately 3,000,000 seniors graduate every year. assuming a 25% drop out rate.

Imagine having 3,000,000 new voters every year who have a good understanding of the philosophical foundation and the Founders' Principles of government for a free people. At this rate, in 10 years we would have 30,000,000 new voters who could change the course of America and put our government back on a set of sound principles.

## 11. Freedom of Religion

Freedom of religion is protected by the First Amendment, but is it really? Religious symbols are generally not allowed in the public squares of America, a place that belongs to all citizens. The citizens clearly have a constitutional right to assemble there peacefully in the name of their religion. School teams are not allowed to pray together while under the sponsorship of the school. No prayer is allowed in school assemblies. No Bible, Torah or Koran is allowed to be read in a public school. No Christmas carols, no Christmas trees, no manger scenes, and no celebration of Hanukkah. A monument displaying the Ten Commandments is forcefully removed from the rotunda of the Alabama Judicial Building and the Chief Justice of the Alabama Supreme Court, who put it there, is removed from office by his own Court. Many other aspects of religion are under attack, including *In God We Trust* on our money, opening Congress with a prayer, and military personnel praying together. Have we gone mad? Surely, the founders of America had nothing like this in mind.

Listen to George Washington in his Farewell Address telling just how important religion is to our country: "…Of all the dispositions and habits, which lead to political prosperity, Religion and morality are indispensable supports…." [22] The Northwest Ordinance (1787),

Article III begins with: "Religion, morality, and knowledge being necessary to good government and the happiness of mankind, schools and the means of education shall forever be encouraged." [23] Thomas Jefferson invited religious groups to assemble on the University of Virginia campus and to use university facilities.

Recommendations:

a) Since all "government property" belongs to the people, and since the people have the constitutional right to assemble there peacefully and the right to speak, they have the right to express their religion on Public Property. (Public Square). Our government has it backwards. They should encourage religious expression, not block it. All religions, except those which embody as part of their belief the destruction of America, should be welcome  Those religions who would kill Americans and destroy America should not be allowed to function at all.

The various religions should take turns with their public displays as assigned by the local government. School classrooms should take turns celebrating each religious holiday, and team prayers should also be passed around. We cannot allow some 5% atheists to dictate to the remaining 95% religionists.

b) Although organizationally separated from it, government should encourage religion. As George Washington said, religion and morality are necessary for "political prosperity."

c) The public displays in government buildings of the Ten Commandments, *In God We Trust*, and other similar statements and quotations should remain there as part of the historical culture of our nation.

12. Only Congress Can Declare War

Article 1, Section 8, Clause 11 of the Constitution states "{ The Congress shall have Power...} To declare War, grant Letters of Marque and Reprisal, and make Rules concerning Captures on Land and Water…." Historically, five wars have been declared in line with this constitutional provision, but beginning with the Korean War ( 1950-1953), no formal declaration of war has been made in connection with the several wars and military interventions in which we have been involved.

In the Constitutional Convention at Philadelphia, only one delegate, Pierce Butler of South Carolina, suggested the President have the power to take the country to war. Elbridge Gerry, delegate from Massachussets, expressed the overwhelming opinion of the Convention when he said "he never expected to hear in a republic a motion to empower the Executive alone to declare war."[30] Nothing so portant as the Declaration of War, which could involve massive loss of life and enormous financial commitments, should be left to the decision of one person.

Following the agonizing experience in the Vietnam War, Congress, in 1973, passed the War Powers Resolution in an attempt to regain its control over the nations' war initiatives. This resolution required the President to consult with Congress BEFORE any troops were committed, and if already engaging in hostilities or likely entering conflict, to file a report to Congress within 48 hours. The troops must be withdrawn within sixty days, with a possible extension of thirty days.

The resolution was passed over President Nixon's veto and every President since has wanted to circumvent it by whatever method was available. For example, President Carter did not even consult with Congress until the "Desert One" hostage rescue episode was over. President Reagan declined to report to Congress after troops were committed in Lebanon in 1982, but he did withdraw all remaining troops before the Resolution's deadline.

In 1986, Reagan used UN Article 51 to justify a tactical air strike against Libya. President George H. W. Bush claimed he did not need any authorization from Congress for the first Gulf War. President Clinton tried to get authorization from the UN Security Council to cover his sending troops to Haiti in 1994. President George W. Bush had to cope with both the War on Terror and the invasion of Iraq. Because of the perceived urgency of both of these wars, the Congress authorized the use of force by the President, but never officially declared war. The requirements of the Constitutional War Powers Clause and the War Powers Resolution were essentially ignored by Congress.[34]

Recommendation:

We must recognize that there has been a substantial change in the nature and means of armed conflict, particularly over the last several decades. Conflict can develop more quickly and decisively now due to several factors, including almost instantaneous communication, the airplane for rapid delivery, the development of nuclear bombs which can obliterate great cities and entire countries with one mortal blow, and the refinement of terrorism which can be swift and deadly. This we experienced in the 9/11/2001 attack on America.

a) At this time the Presidency seems to have an upper hand in the Declaration of War debate with Congress, although the President alone must not be allowed to make that decision.

b) The Congress must develop a stiff back and openly insist on the President's acting within the provisions of the War Powers Resolution. That could cause an open conflict between the President and Congress, but so be it.

c) The Congress must develop an environment wherein the President is expected to observe the rules.

d) The Congress should act more often on its prerogative to declare war. The war with Iraq is a good example. It would be a strong psychological move.

e) It could certainly help if America would stop trying to be the world's policeman and defender.

## 13. American Sovereignty and Foreign Entanglements

The concerns here go back to the earliest times in our nation, when in his 1796 Farewell Address, President George Washington warned in the strongest terms of the dangers of entanglements with foreign nations. He said, " The great rule of conduct for us, in regard to foreign nations, is in extending our commercial relations to have with them as little political connection as possible …. It is our true policy to steer clear of permanent alliances with any portion of the foreign world."[24] This policy is not to be found in the Constitution but was the good judgment of the Founders themselves.Washington's statement was followed just four years later by President Thomas Jefferson, who said in his First Inaugural Address : "… peace, commerce, and honest friendship with all nations, entangling alliances with none."[25] Although we may agree these are sound policies, living by them in a world going global can be very difficult. It is easy to yield first an inch, then a yard, and finally a mile, until we realize we have established a relationship very dangerous to our sovereignty. Consider the following:

Already 157 nations have signed onto the 1982 UN Law of the *Sea Treaty* which will control, under a UN bureaucracy, fishing rights, navigation lanes, and the ocean bed's oil and mineral resources in all global international waters.

The *World Court*, also known as the *International Court of Justice*, was established in 1945. "As stated in Article 93 of the UN Charter, all 192 members of the UN are automatically parties to the Court's statute." The United States agreed to its compulsory jurisdiction until 1984 when the U. S. withdrew this acceptance as a result of the Court, in *Nicaragua vs United States*, deciding that the U.S. had employed "unlawful use of force" against Nicaragua. The Court "…ordered the U. S. to pay war reparations…" to Nicaragua.

The *UN Climate Change Treaty* is being given much attention these days as demonstrated at the recent Copenhaven Conference, where our President made strong commitments of support and leadership by the United States to make it happen. This treaty centers on limiting the amount of $CO_2$ emitted into the atmosphere by requiring a drastic reduction in energy consumption. This is the energy produced by the fossil fuels, oil, coal, and natural gas. Even our President predicts large increases in energy costs. This will result in a lowered standard of living for the people. I must point out that the science underlying this movement is in serious question, both in the pure science itself and in the integrity of some of the key scientists pushing it.

Then there is the *UN Comprehensive Nuclear Test Ban Treaty*, the *UN Treaty on Women*, and the *UN Treaty on the Rights of the Child.*

In addition to these treaties, we now have the Global Tax idea floating around the United Nations again. A strong proponent is former Secretary-General, Kofi Annan. This is a worldwide tax to support the UN and its programs. A new study is preparing various proposals to be considered at next September's meeting of the General Assembly. One of the primary goals of this movement is to redistribute the wealth of the richer nations to poorer nations in the third world. (Where have we heard that word "redistribution" before?) The sources for this additional global tax income are to be things like emails at $0.01 per each megabyte of data to yield some $150 billion per year; a tax on fossil fuels like gasoline, coal, oil and natural gas to yield some $125 billion per year; a tax on all currency transactions of 0.1 % for each transaction to yield some $264 billion per year, and other similar sources.[31] The United States already pays the lion's share of the annual dues paid to the UN.

All of these treaties create massive international bureaucracies, and as Phyllis Schlafly reports, "Every UN treaty would interfere with self-government over some aspect of our lives and would transfer significant power to foreign bureaucracies, many of whom hate and envy America."[32]

While some presidents have signed onto certain of these treaties, so far the Senate has had the good judgment to refuse permanent approval of any of them. (As previously reported, the U. S. did agree early on to the compulsory jurisdiction of the World Court but later withdrew its acceptance). However, great pressures are building among both Senate and administrative leadership for us to become a team player in the so-called "world community."

The reason this matter of treaties is so critical is that our constitution states in Article VI, Item 2, that "This Constitution and the Laws of the United States…; and all Treaties made…, shall be the Supreme Law of the Land…." Because of this constitutional provision, we must be extremely careful what obligations of a foreign nature we take on.

In a different mode from the treaties of the UN , which are the greatest concern, is the very disturbing development known as The Security and Prosperity Partnership of North America (SPP). This Partnership was announced by President Bush in March 2005. It includes the United States, Canada, and Mexico and commits the United States to "hemispheric integration." Bush was very cautious in describing the goals of the SPP, using code words like "economic integration" and "labor mobility." According to the Eagle Forum, "The CFR (Council on Foreign Relations) Report of May 17, 2005, posted on the U. S. State Department website, states that the 3 SPP amigos (President George Bush, Mexican President Vicente Fox, and Canadian Prime Minister Paul Martin) at Waco on March 23, 2005 'committed their governments' to 'Building a North American Community' by 2010…. " [26]

The Security and Prosperity Partnership of North America seems to be developing in an entirely different way than the treaties and agreements of the UN. Much is said about the various conventions of the UN, but seldom do we see or read anything about the SPP. It's almost as though it is a "stealth project," which serves to make it even more ominous and suspicious. Perhaps the proponents of this have plans to work it so that the Senate does not get to review and vote on the project.

Peter F. Drucker, a noted consultant to business and industry, said in his Post-Capitalist Society:"...the economic integration of the three countries (U.S., Mexico, and Canada) into one region is proceeding so fast that it will make little difference whether the marriage is sanctified legally or not."[33]

Dr. Daneen Peterson, in a speech in Washington, June 15, 2007, declared that "...our government is illegally creating the NAU (North American Union) by using secret meetings and deceptive double-speak to hide their treasonous, incremental stealth. They are making MASSIVE changes to our regulatory laws and calling them 'harmonizations'. What they are doing is degrading 200 years of our nation's administrative law. They are rewriting our regulatory law, which involves every facet of our daily lives, in order to integrate our laws with Mexico's corrupt oligarchy and Canada's socialist parliamentary system." [27] Does one need to wonder why the United States has built only 18 miles of the 854 miles of double fence authorized by Congress along our southern border? The fence would be in the way if we are going to integrate the two nations.

Finally, take the case of Michael New.[28] He joined the army in 1993, taking an oath to defend the Constitution of the United States. Nothing was said to him at the time about any connection with the United Nations or any foreign power. He was assigned to Germany. Sometime after his arrival there, his battalion was ordered to put on a United Nations uniform as they were to be deployed in a United Nations peacekeeping mission to Macedonia. His unit was commanded by a Finnish General of the United Nations. New refused to put on the uniform, as his oath was to serve the U. S., not the U.N. The case attracted national attention, and after numerous court proceedings, Michael New was given a Bad Conduct Discharge in January, 1996. Finally, eleven years later, the Supreme Court refused to hear the case. This case opens a number of questions about American sovereignty.

Of all abuses, those of sovereignty are some of the most serious and difficult problems facing us. There are today powerful forces at work, in both the United States and a number of the leading countries of the world, who are trying to set up a New World Order consisting of a one world government over all nations. We should never be a part of any such New World Order. American sovereignty must always be paramount. We can be interested only in cooperation, never subjugation. There can be no doubt that the long term protection of America's sovereignty is, and will continue to be, a subject of major and pressing concern.

Recommendations:

The recommendations that follow are not intended to be isolationist or imperialist. They are intended to protect the sovereignty of this nation, while being commercially strong, humanitarian, helpful, and cooperative, but not politically entangling. Do we have the courage and the will to do these things?

a) Lead the world by example, by quality of our national character, by being the envy of the world, by helping other nations in times of disaster and illness, and in teaching them how to help themselves.

b) Maintain, as nearly as possible, the guideline recommended by Thomas Jefferson, "…peace, commerce, and honest friendship with all nations, entangling alliances with none." [25]

c) Maintain the world's strongest, most advanced military for defense, not aggression .

d) Stop illegal immigration. Build the fence across our southern border.

e) Stop trying to be the world's policeman and the world's defender. We can't afford such action, and it tends to drag us into military conflict.

f) Refuse any subjugation of American independence and rights to the United Nations.

g) Establish within the United Nations a group of nations who believe in, and practice, human rights and government of and by the people.

h) Allow only volunteers among American military personnel to serve under the United Nations. Recognize Michael New with a full honorable discharge.

i) Stop the formation of the North American Community, one of the most immediate dangers to American sovereignty.

j) Counteract all efforts to lead us into a one world government, or any encroachment on our independence from foreign intrusion. As with the North American Union, there would then be no more America as we have known it.

k) Consider carefully the positives and negatives of withdrawing the United States' membership in the United Nations.

\* \* \* \* \* \* \* \* \*

Our failure to follow the Constitution and Founders' Principles has been going on for many decades, but it has taken on a new velocity and aggressiveness in recent administrations. Our leaders now seem determined to change America in fundamental ways contrary to the American way—from freedom of the individual to a statist, socialist form of government, where the elite think they are more capable in deciding what the people need than the people are in deciding for themselves.

America is at a frightening crossroads. Either we move toward ever more government control over our lives, or we turn once again toward strong, individual freedom. There is a common saying that when all else fails, go back to the original instructions ... our original instructions are found in **The Declaration of Independence, the United States Constitution, and the Founders' Principles.**

The premise of this book is that the only intelligent and safe choice is to  restore the Great American Dream by rediscovering the philosophical foundations and Founders' Principles of government for a free people. **It is our belief that the principles that made America great are the same principles that will keep America great**, and if we fail to understand that, our America will be changed forever. As Madison stated, "…every word (of the Constitution) decides a question between power and liberty…." [29] Today we are facing the choice between power and liberty all over again.

Americans must forget for now being a Republican or a Democrat. We must first learn how to *be* AMERICAN, *think* AMERICAN, and especially, *act* AMERICAN— not by the end of the year, not next week, but now. Or, to put it another way, stop thinking Party per se, and start thinking Constitution and Principles, for THEY ARE the American way.

In a nutshell, our philosophical foundations, the Founders' Principles of government for a free people, and the spirit that emanates from them, constitute the heart and soul of America and are the basis for the Great American Dream.

***The Dream* is the open door to personal achievement, limited only by one's abilities and determination**. Historically, this opportunity has been possible only in America.

The philosophy and the principles needed for the road back are presented in this book. They are our guide. They are our measuring stick. We must rediscover these foundations and principles before it is too late, if we hope to save our great nation, if we hope to save the heart and soul of America, if we hope to re-ignite in full force The Great American Dream.

I hope you will read carefully, think deeply, and ACT on this great challenge. America desperately needs you to do your part.

# Chapter 5

# General Suggestions For Actions
## To Save
## "The Great American Dream"

It is one thing to be interested in a cause, to think about it in depth, or to talk about it. However, it is quite another thing to act decisively and meaningfully. The Great American Dream is under assault today. The heart and soul of America are under assault. The entire industrial and financial structure of America is under assault. Our religion is under assault. We are being driven toward some sort of statist, socialist society which, if it happens, will surely destroy The Great American Dream.

Your interest and ACTION are needed at this very moment. Anyone and everyone can and must help. Our goals must be designed for both short and long term.

Short term

• Our first job is to vote out all politicians, local, state, and federal, who work against the founding philosophy and principles of our country.

• It is also our job to work against any current legislation or political moves that are contrary to our founding principles.

Long term

Educate the American people, especially our young people, about our philosophy and principles of government for a free people. A formalized semester course on these principles is currently in development, and you can be very helpful in getting this course taught in your local high school. (See item #11)

Here are some suggestions on the actions to be taken. This is certainly not an exhaustive list, but, hopefully, it constitutes a good start.

REMEMBER, THE STAKES ARE VERY HIGH.

## 1. Educate Yourself On Our Form of Government

The first things you need to know and understand are the philosophical foundations and the Founders' Principles of government for a free people. This book explains these things in Chapter 2 and Chapter 4 shows the way back. Share this book with others. Form a family or neighborhood study group and enjoy the learning process together.

## 2. Educate others

If you are a business owner, manager, or a leader of an organization, consider giving a copy of this book to each of your employees or associates (volume prices are available). They need to know these fundamentals of our form of government. The reason our country faces its massive problems today is because the citizens were never taught the principles of government for a free people. Do all you can to spread the word.

## 3. Know What's Going On

Keep current on legislation and government actions that do harm to our heritage of freedom. Only with this knowledge can you move in the most needed and advantageous ways. Some suggestions on how to do this:

a) Join The Heritage Foundation for their regular updates.

214 Massachusetts Avenue NE

Washington, D. C. 20002-4999

b) Join The Eagle Forum for excellent reports from attorney Phyllis Schlafly.

P. O. Box 818

Alton, IL 62002

c) Consider subscriptions to the following, which together, will eveal the arguments from all sides:

1. Wall Street Journal
2. Human Events
3. The Weekly Standard

4. American Spectator
5. The New York Times
6. The Washington Post

7. The Washington Times

4. Know How Your Representatives Plan To Vote On Our Special Issues

Knowing this information as early as possible gives you more time to influence votes. Get updates on special issues by calling either their state office or Washington office.

5. Contact Your Senators and Congressman

Personal, face to face conversation is always the best when you are trying to influence a vote. If this is not possible, call, write, or fax both their Washington and State offices. Prepare a list of all contact information for each representative, for both their Washington and all State offices. In the case of Congressmen, it's a good idea to have this information for all state representatives. Although there is only one Congressman in your district, there may be times when it will be helpful to write your entire state delegation.

6. Organize Neighborhood Groups

You will discover you are not alone in your concerns about our America. A group can almost always exert more pressure on politicians than a single individual. A neighborhood group will be especially effective for local and state elections and pressure between elections. Hold Block Parties occasionally as needed.

7. Actively support Good Representatives Already in Office

All representatives who currently vote in keeping with the Founders' Principles should be supported. Contact their local office and ask what you can do to help. This is especially important at least a year before the next election.

## 8. Search For Outstanding Candidates

The key to responsible government is to elect the right representatives in the first place. Work at all levels, beginning with your School Board and City Council. Be sure the candidates believe in, and will support, the Founders' principles and philosophy.

## 9. Attend Town Hall Meetings

Speak out. Be courteous, but be bold and firm. Take a friend with you. The outstanding success of this year's Town Hall meetings is powerful testimony to how effective this approach can be.

## 10. Support the Tea Parties

Do all you can to support the Tea Parties to keep them vital and effective until the next election, which will be the first real opportunity to change the players in Washington. The Tea Parties and their fallout are essential to our getting America back on the right track.

## 11. Education—Vitally Important For the Long Term

Your neighborhood group can be especially effective when they go into the schools and find what is, and is not, being taught to their children.

Start a movement in your state to enact legislation requiring the teaching of a full semester course on the Founders' Principles of government for a free people. Make a passing grade in the semester course mandatory for high school graduation. **A sample of such a bill is found in the Appendix of this book**. A bill like this will be introduced in the next session of the General Assembly of North Carolina. A Semester Course will be available in complete detail for the teacher, lesson by lesson by the time the legislation is enacted. This is one of the most important actions you can take.

While it doesn't solve the immediate problems, it profoundly addresses the long term problem in America, especially in educating the future voters of our country.

12. Letters To the Editor

Write meaningful and persuasive Letters to the Editor in an effort to educate others about the importance of the cause of saving America. Program your computer to send your letters to ALL the newspapers in your state by punching only one key. For Outlook Express, here is what you do:

a) Through Google, search for a list of all cities in your State with a population of 5,000 or more.

b) Compile this list on a spread sheet.

c). Go on line to each city and find the name and email address of their newspaper.(s)

d) Google each newspaper for its email address for the Letters to the Editor.

e). Compile a list of these addresses in your Group Contact file in your email program.

f) Give the Group File a name, such as NEWSPAPERS. This is a permanent file.

g) Write your letter, click on NEWSPAPERS, and send your message to all listed newspapers with one click.

This is a wonderful way to get your message out to millions of people. The downside of this is that you will not know how many newspapers printed the letter.

13. Articles For the Op/Ed Page

Write articles for the Op/Ed Editor and submit them in the same way as in #12 above.

14. The Silent Majority Must Speak Out

If you are a member of the vast silent majority, you can no longer afford to be silent. This is the time you MUST be vocal.

15. Moms Need To Organize

Moms can be powerful, especially when they are organized. If you are a Mom and want to help, one of the neatest things you can do is to join with one of these national programs. Try asamom.org

16. Work Hard and Pray

Although intensified in recent years, the abuse of our Constitution and the Founders' Principles has been going on for a long time. Extraordinary effort will be required to restore our America, so work hard, keep pushing, and don't give up. Also, remember, our inalienable rights come from God, so pray hard for our cause.

17. VOTE

18. Funding

Serious funding is needed. For those of you who are in position to make cash contributions, please do so. There are many organizations operating in the fight to restore America and protect The Great American Dream. We list here only a few with whom we have personally worked or who have operations based on the Founders' Principles:

a) The Bill of Rights Institute

200 North Glebe Road Suite 200

Arlington, VA 22203

703-894-1776

b) The Heritage Foundation

214 Massachusetts Avenue , NW

Washington, D. C. 20002-4999

202-546-4400

c) The Federalist Society

015 18th Street, NW Suite 425

Washington, D.C. 20036

202-822-8138

d) National Center for Constitutional Studies

37777 Juniper Road

Malta, ID 83342

208-645-2625

e) Intercollegiate Studies Institute, Inc.

3901 Centerville Road

Wilmington, DE 19807-1938

302-652-4600

# APPENDIX

## Declaration of Independence
(Underlined for special emphasis)

## United States Constitution

Thomas Jefferson

*Author of the*

## Declaration of Independence

**Third President of the United States**

# Declaration Of Independence

## In Congress, July 4, 1776.

*THE UNANIMOUS DECLARATION OF THE THIRTEEN UNITED STATES OF AMERICA (EMPHASIS ADDED)*

When in the Course of human events it becomes necessary for one people to dissolve the political bands which have connected them with another, and to assume among the powers of the earth, the separate and equal station to which the Laws of Nature and of Nature's God entitle them, a decent respect to the opinions of mankind requires that they should declare the causes which impel them to the separation. – We hold these truths to be self-evident, that all men are created equal, that they are endowed by their Creator with certain unalienable Rights, that among these are Life, Liberty and the pursuit of Happiness. That to secure these rights, Governments are instituted among Men, deriving their just powers from the consent of the governed, That whenever any Form of Government becomes destructive of these ends, it is the Right of the People to alter or to abolish it, and to institute new Government, laying its foundation on such principles and organizing its powers in such form, as to them shall seem most likely to effect their Safety and Happiness. Prudence, indeed, will dictate that Governments long established should not be changed for light and transient causes; and accordingly all experience hath shown, that mankind are more disposed to suffer, while evils are sufferable, than to right themselves by abolishing the forms to which they are accustomed. But when a long train of abuses and usurpations, pursuing invariably the same Object evinces a design to reduce them under absolute Despotism, it is their right, it is their duty, to throw off such Government, and to provide new Guards for their future security. – Such has been the patient sufferance of these Colonies; and such is now the necessity which constrains them to alter their former Systems of Government. The history of the present King of Great Britain is a history of repeated injuries and usurpations, all having in direct object the establishment of an absolute Tyranny over these States. To prove this, let Facts be submitted to a candid world. – He has refused his Assent to Laws, the most wholesome and necessary for the public good. – He has forbidden his Governors to pass Laws of immediate and pressing importance, unless suspended in their operation till his Assent should be obtained; and when so suspended, he has utterly neglected to attend to them. – He has refused to pass other Laws for the accommodation of large districts of people, unless those people would relinquish the right of Representation in the Legislature, a right inestimable to them and formidable to tyrants only. – He has called together legislative bodies at places unusual, uncomfortable, and distant from the depository of their public Records, for the sole purpose of fatiguing them into compliance with his measures. – He has dissolved Representative Houses repeatedly, for opposing with manly firmness his invasions on the rights of the people. – He has refused for a long time, after such dissolutions, to cause others to be elected; whereby the Legislative powers, incapable of Annihilation, have returned to the People at large for their exercise; the State remaining in the mean time exposed to all the dangers of invasion from without, and convulsions within. – He has endeavoured to prevent the population of these States; for that purpose obstructing the Laws for Naturalization of Foreigners; refusing to pass others to encourage their migrations hither, and raising the conditions of new Appropriations of Lands. – He has obstructed the Administration of Justice, by refusing his Assent to Laws for establishing Judiciary powers. – He has made Judges dependent on his Will alone, for the tenure of their offices, and the amount and payment of their salaries. – He has erected a multitude of New Offices, and sent hither swarms of Officers to harass our people, and eat out their substance. – He has kept among us, in times of peace, Standing Armies without the Consent of our legislatures. – He has affected to render the Military independent of and superior to the Civil power. – He has combined with others to subject us to a jurisdiction foreign to our constitution, and unacknowledged by our laws; giving his Assent to their Acts of pretended Legislation: – For quartering large bodies of armed troops among us: – For protecting them, by a mock Trial, from punishment for any Murders which they should commit on the Inhabitants of these States: – For cutting off our Trade with all parts of the world: – For imposing taxes on us without our Consent: For depriving us in many cases, of the benefits of Trial by Jury: – For transporting us beyond Seas to be tried for pretended offenses: – For abolishing the free System of English Laws in a neighbouring Province, establishing therein an Arbitrary government, and enlarging its Boundaries so as to render it at once an example and fit instrument for introducing the same absolute rule into these Colonies: – For taking away our Charters, abolishing our most valuable Laws and altering fundamentally the Forms of our Governments: –For suspending our own Legislatures, and declaring themselves invested with power to legislate for us in all cases whatsoever. He has abdicated Government here, by declaring us out of his Protection and waging War against us. – He has plundered our seas, ravaged our Coasts, burnt our towns, and destroyed the lives of our people. – He is at this time transporting large Armies of foreign Mercenaries to compleat the works of death, desolation and tyranny, already begun with circumstances of Cruelty & perfidy scarcely paralleled in the most barbarous ages, and totally unworthy the Head of a civilized nation. – He has constrained our fellow Citizens taken Captive on the high Seas to bear Arms against their Country, to become the executioners of their friends and Brethren, or to fall themselves by their Hands. – He has excited domestic insurrections amongst us, and has endeavoured to bring on the inhabitants of our frontiers, the merciless Indian Savages, whose known rule of warfare, is an undistinguished destruction of all ages, sexes and conditions. – In every stage of these Oppressions We have Petitioned for Redress in the most humble terms: Our repeated Petitions have been answered only by repeated injury. A Prince, whose character is thus marked by every act which may define a Tyrant, is unfit to be the ruler of a free people. – Nor have We been wanting in attentions to our British brethren. We have warned them from time to time of attempts by their legislature to extend an unwarrantable jurisdiction over us. We have reminded them of the circumstances of our emigration and settlement here. We have appealed to their native justice and magnanimity, and we have conjured them by the ties of our common kindred to disavow these ursurpations, which would inevitably interrupt our connections and correspondence. They too have been deaf to the voice of justice and of consanguinity. We must, therefore, acquiesce in the necessity, which denounces our Separation, and hold them, as we hold the rest of mankind, Enemies in War, in Peace Friends.

We, therefore, the Representatives of the United States of America, in General Congress, Assembled, appealing to the Supreme Judge of the world for the rectitude of our intentions, do, in the Name, and by Authority of the good People of these Colonies, solemnly publish and declare, That these United Colonies are, and of Right ought to be Free and Independent States; that they are Absolved from all Allegiance to the British Crown, and that all political connection between them and the State of Great Britian, is and ought to be totally dissolved; and that as Free and Independent States, they have full Power to levy War, conclude Peace, contract Alliances, establish Commerce, and to do all other Acts and Things which Independent States may of right do. And for the support of this Declaration, with a firm reliance on the protection of divine Providence, we mutually pledge to each other our Lives, our Fortunes and our sacred Honor.

*(Connecticut)*
Roger Sherman
Sam'el Huntington
Wm. Williams
Oliver Wolcott

*(Delaware)*
Caesar Rodney
Geo. Read
Tho. M'Kean

*(Georgia)*
Button Gwinnett
Lyman Hall
Geo. Walton

*(Maryland)*
Samuel Chase
Wm. Paca

Thos. Stone
Charles Carroll of
   Carrollton

*(Massachusetts)*
John Hancock
Saml. Adams
John Adams
Robt. Treat Paine
Elbridge Gerry

*(New Hampshire)*
Josiah Bartlett
Wm. Whipple
Matthew Thornton

*(New Jersey)*
Richd. Stockton
Jno Witherspoon
Fras. Hopkinson
John Hart
Abra. Clark

*(New York)*
Wm. Floyd
Phil. Livingston
Frans. Lewis
Lewis Morris

*(North Carolina)*
Wm. Hooper
Joseph Hewes
John Penn

*(Pennsylvania)*
Robt. Morris
Benjamin Rush
Benja. Franklin
John Morton
Geo. Clymer
Jas. Smith
Geo. Taylor

James Wilson
Geo. Ross

*(Rhode Island)*
Step. Hopkins
William Ellery

*(South Carolina)*
Edward Rutledge
Thos. Heyward, Junr.
Thomas Lynch, Junr.
Arthur Middleton

*(Virginia)*
George Wythe
Richard Henry Lee
Th. Jefferson
Benja. Harrison
Thos. Nelson, jr.
Francis Lightfoot Lee
Carter Braxton

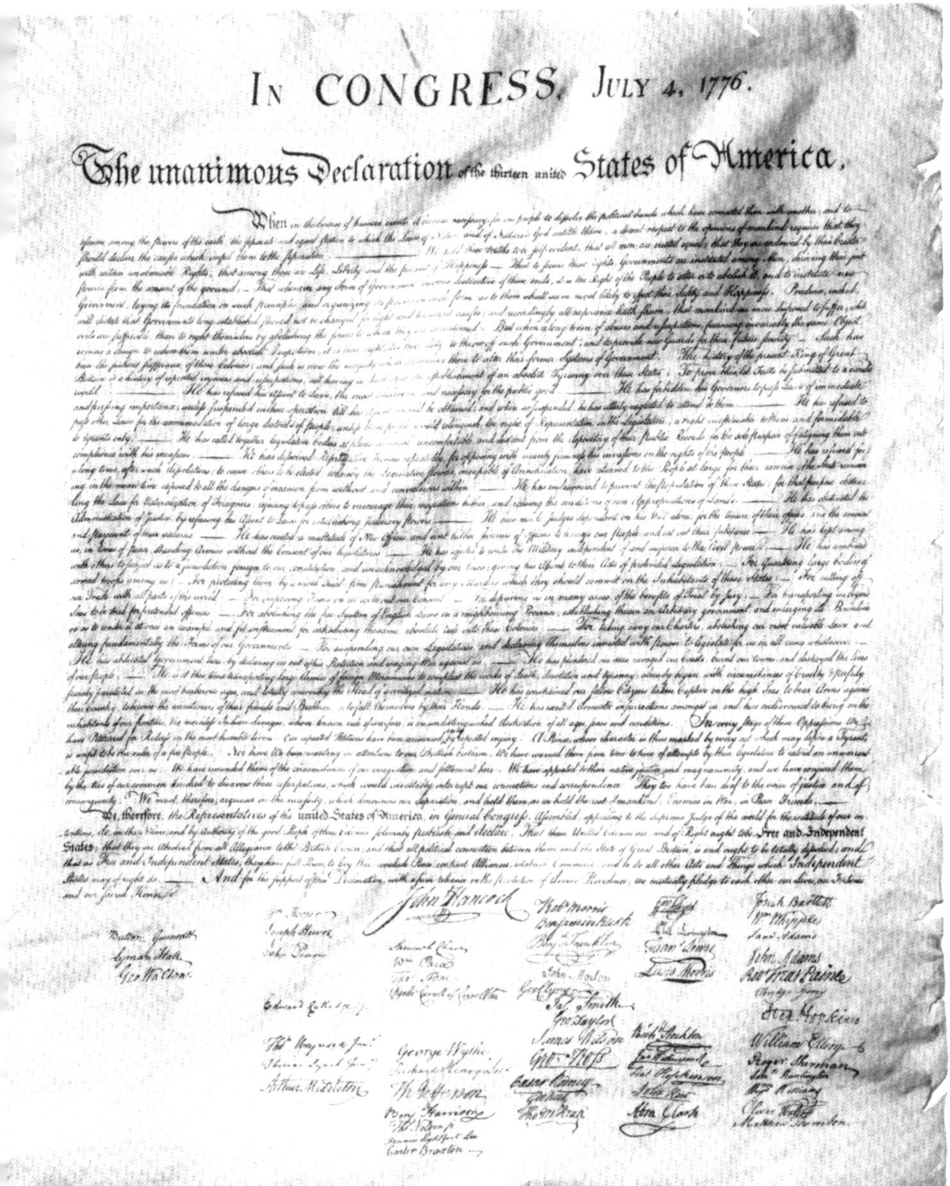

IN CONGRESS, JULY 4, 1776.

The unanimous Declaration of the thirteen united States of America,

When in the Course of human events, it becomes necessary for one people to dissolve the political bands which have connected them with another, and to assume among the powers of the earth, the separate and equal station to which the Laws of Nature and of Nature's God entitle them, a decent respect to the opinions of mankind requires that they should declare the causes which impel them to the separation. — We hold these truths to be self-evident, that all men are created equal, that they are endowed by their Creator with certain unalienable Rights, that among these are Life, Liberty and the pursuit of Happiness. — That to secure these rights, Governments are instituted among Men, deriving their just powers from the consent of the governed, — That whenever any Form of Government becomes destructive of these ends, it is the Right of the People to alter or to abolish it, and to institute new Government, laying its foundation on such principles and organizing its powers in such form, as to them shall seem most likely to effect their Safety and Happiness. Prudence, indeed, will dictate that Governments long established should not be changed for light and transient causes; and accordingly all experience hath shewn, that mankind are more disposed to suffer, while evils are sufferable, than to right themselves by abolishing the forms to which they are accustomed. But when a long train of abuses and usurpations, pursuing invariably the same Object evinces a design to reduce them under absolute Despotism, it is their right, it is their duty, to throw off such Government, and to provide new Guards for their future security. — Such has been the patient sufferance of these Colonies; and such is now the necessity which constrains them to alter their former Systems of Government. The history of the present King of Great Britain is a history of repeated injuries and usurpations, all having in direct object the establishment of an absolute Tyranny over these States. To prove this, let Facts be submitted to a candid world. — He has refused his Assent to Laws, the most wholesome and necessary for the public good. — He has forbidden his Governors to pass Laws of immediate and pressing importance, unless suspended in their operation till his Assent should be obtained; and when so suspended, he has utterly neglected to attend to them. — He has refused to pass other Laws for the accommodation of large districts of people, unless those people would relinquish the right of Representation in the Legislature, a right inestimable to them and formidable to tyrants only. — He has called together legislative bodies at places unusual, uncomfortable, and distant from the depository of their public Records, for the sole purpose of fatiguing them into compliance with his measures. — He has dissolved Representative Houses repeatedly, for opposing with manly firmness his invasions on the rights of the people. — He has refused for a long time, after such dissolutions, to cause others to be elected; whereby the Legislative powers, incapable of Annihilation, have returned to the People at large for their exercise; the State remaining in the mean time exposed to all the dangers of invasion from without, and convulsions within. — He has endeavoured to prevent the population of these States; for that purpose obstructing the Laws for Naturalization of Foreigners; refusing to pass others to encourage their migrations hither, and raising the conditions of new Appropriations of Lands. — He has obstructed the Administration of Justice, by refusing his Assent to Laws for establishing Judiciary powers. — He has made Judges dependent on his Will alone, for the tenure of their offices, and the amount and payment of their salaries. — He has erected a multitude of New Offices, and sent hither swarms of Officers to harrass our people, and eat out their substance. — He has kept among us, in times of peace, Standing Armies without the Consent of our legislatures. — He has affected to render the Military independent of and superior to the Civil power. — He has combined with others to subject us to a jurisdiction foreign to our constitution, and unacknowledged by our laws; giving his Assent to their Acts of pretended Legislation: — For Quartering large bodies of armed troops among us: — For protecting them, by a mock Trial, from punishment for any Murders which they should commit on the Inhabitants of these States: — For cutting off our Trade with all parts of the world: — For imposing Taxes on us without our Consent: — For depriving us in many cases, of the benefits of Trial by Jury: — For transporting us beyond Seas to be tried for pretended offences — For abolishing the free System of English Laws in a neighbouring Province, establishing therein an Arbitrary government, and enlarging its Boundaries so as to render it at once an example and fit instrument for introducing the same absolute rule into these Colonies: — For taking away our Charters, abolishing our most valuable Laws, and altering fundamentally the Forms of our Governments: — For suspending our own Legislatures, and declaring themselves invested with power to legislate for us in all cases whatsoever. — He has abdicated Government here, by declaring us out of his Protection and waging War against us. — He has plundered our seas, ravaged our Coasts, burnt our towns, and destroyed the lives of our people. — He is at this time transporting large Armies of foreign Mercenaries to compleat the works of death, desolation and tyranny, already begun with circumstances of Cruelty & perfidy scarcely paralleled in the most barbarous ages, and totally unworthy the Head of a civilized nation. — He has constrained our fellow Citizens taken Captive on the high Seas to bear Arms against their Country, to become the executioners of their friends and Brethren, or to fall themselves by their Hands. — He has excited domestic insurrections amongst us, and has endeavoured to bring on the inhabitants of our frontiers, the merciless Indian Savages, whose known rule of warfare, is an undistinguished destruction of all ages, sexes and conditions. In every stage of these Oppressions We have Petitioned for Redress in the most humble terms: Our repeated Petitions have been answered only by repeated injury. A Prince, whose character is thus marked by every act which may define a Tyrant, is unfit to be the ruler of a free people. Nor have We been wanting in attentions to our British brethren. We have warned them from time to time of attempts by their legislature to extend an unwarrantable jurisdiction over us. We have reminded them of the circumstances of our emigration and settlement here. We have appealed to their native justice and magnanimity, and we have conjured them by the ties of our common kindred to disavow these usurpations, which would inevitably interrupt our connections and correspondence. They too have been deaf to the voice of justice and of consanguinity. We must, therefore, acquiesce in the necessity, which denounces our Separation, and hold them, as we hold the rest of mankind, Enemies in War, in Peace Friends.

We, therefore, the Representatives of the united States of America, in General Congress, Assembled, appealing to the Supreme Judge of the world for the rectitude of our intentions, do, in the Name, and by Authority of the good People of these Colonies, solemnly publish and declare, That these United Colonies are, and of Right ought to be Free and Independent States; that they are Absolved from all Allegiance to the British Crown, and that all political connection between them and the State of Great Britain, is and ought to be totally dissolved; and that as Free and Independent States, they have full Power to levy War, conclude Peace, contract Alliances, establish Commerce, and to do all other Acts and Things which Independent States may of right do. — And for the support of this Declaration, with a firm reliance on the protection of divine Providence, we mutually pledge to each other our Lives, our Fortunes and our sacred Honor.

John Hancock

James Madison
*known as*
**The Father Of The Constitution**

Fourth President of the United States

# CONSTITUTION

## of the

## United States of America

"We the People of the United States, in Order to form a
more perfect Union, establish Justice, insure domestic Tranquility, provide
for the common defence, promote the general Welfare, and secure the
Blessings of Liberty to ourselves and our Posterity, do ordain and establish
this Constitution for the United States of America."

"The Most Wonderful Work Ever Struck Off At A Given Time
By The Brain And Purpose Of Man."

– William E. Gladstone (1809-1898)
*British Prime Minister & Statesman*

## Article I

### Section 1

All legislative Powers herein granted shall be vested in a Congress of the United States, which shall consist of a Senate and House of Representatives.

### Section 2

(1) The House of Representatives shall be composed of Members chosen every second Year by the People of the several States, and the Electors in each State shall have the Qualifications requisite for Electors of the most numerous Branch of the State Legislature.

(2) No Person shall be a Representative who shall not have attained to the Age of twenty five Years, and been seven Years a Citizen of the United States, and who shall not, when elected, be an Inhabitant of that State in which he shall be chosen.

(3) Representatives and direct Taxes shall be apportioned among the several States which may be included within this Union, according to their respective Numbers, which shall be determined by adding to the whole Number of free Persons, including those bound to Service for a Term of Years, and excluding Indians not taxed, three fifths of all other Persons. The actual Enumeration shall be made within three Years after the first Meeting of the Congress of the United States, and within every subsequent Term often Years, in such Manner as they shall by Law direct. The Number of Representatives shall not exceed one for every thirty Thousand, but each State shall have at Least one Representative; and until such enumeration shall be made, the State of New Hampshire shall be entitled to chuse three, Massachusetts eight, Rhode Island and Providence Plantations one, Connecticut five, New York six, New Jersey four, Pennsylvania eight, Delaware one, Maryland six, Virginia ten, North Carolina five, South Carolina five, and Georgia three.

(4) When vacancies happen in the Representation from any State, the Executive Authority thereof shall issue Writs of Election to fill such Vacancies.

(5) The House of Representatives shall chuse their speaker and other Officers; and shall have the sole Power of Impeachment.

### Section 3

(1) The Senate of the United States shall be composed of two Senators from each State, chosen by the Legislature thereof, for six Years; and each Senator shall have one Vote.

(2) Immediately after they shall be assembled in Consequence of the first Election, they shall be divided as equally as may be into three Classes. The Seats of the Senators of the first Class shall be vacated at the Expiration of the second Year, of the second Class at the Expiration of the fourth Year, and of the third Class at the Expiration of the sixth Year, so that one third may be chosen every second Year; and if Vacancies happen by Resignation, or otherwise, during the Recess of the Legislature of any State, the Executive thereof may make temporary Appointments until the next Meeting of the Legislature, which shall then fill such Vacancies.

(3) No Person shall be a Senator who shall not have attained to the Age of thirty Years, and been nine Years a Citizen of the United States, and who shall not, when elected, be an Inhabitant of that State for which he shall be chosen.

(4) The Vice President of the United States shall be President of the Senate, but

shall have no Vote, unless they be equally divided.

(5) The Senate shall chuse their other Officers, and also a President pro tempore, in the Absence of the Vice President, or when he shall exercise the Office of President of the United States.

(6) The Senate shall have the sole Power to try all Impeachments. When sitting for that Purpose, they shall be on Oath or Affirmation. When the President of the United States is tried, the Chief Justice shall preside: And no Person shall be convicted without the Concurrence of two-thirds of the Members present.

(7) Judgment in Cases of Impeachment shall not extend further than to removal from Office, and disqualification to hold and enjoy any Office of honor, Trust or Profit under the United States; but the Party convicted shall nevertheless be liable and subject to Indictment, Trial, Judgment and Punishment, according to law.

## Section 4

(1) The Times, Places and Manner of holding Elections for Senators and Representatives, shall be prescribed in each State by the Legislature thereof; but the Congress may at any time by Law make or alter such Regulations, except as to the Places of chusing Senators.

(2) The Congress shall assemble at least once in every Year, and such Meeting shall be on the first Monday in December, unless they shall by Law appoint a different Day.

## Section 5

(1) Each House shall be the judge of the Elections, Returns and Qualifications of its own Members, and a Majority of each shall constitute a Quorum to do Business; but a smaller Number may adjourn from day to day, and may be authorized to compel the Attendance of absent Members, in such Manner, and under such Penalties as each House may provide.

(2) Each House may determine the Rules of its Proceedings, punish its Members for disorderly Behaviour, and, with the Concurrence of two thirds, expel a Member.

(3) Each House shall keep a Journal of its Proceedings, and from time to time publish the same, excepting such Parts as may in their Judgment require Secrecy; and the Yeas and Nays of the Members of either House on any question shall, at the Desire of one fifth of those Present, be entered on the Journal.

(4) Neither House, during the Session of Congress, shall, without the Consent of the other, adjourn for more than three days, nor to any other place than that in which the two Houses shall be sitting.

## Section 6

(1) The Senators and Representatives shall receive a Compensation for their Services, to be ascertained by Law, and paid out of the Treasury of the United States, They shall in all Cases, except Treason, Felony and Breach of the Peace, be privileged from Arrest during their Attendance at the Session of their respective Houses, and in going to and returning from the same; and for any Speech or Debate in either House, they shall not be questioned in any other Place.

(2) No Senator or Representative shall, during the Time for which he was elected, be appointed to any civil Office under the Authority of the United States, which shall have been created, or the Emoluments whereof shall have been encreased during such time; and no Person holding any Office under the United States, shall be a Member of either House during his Continuance in Office.

## Section 7

(1) All Bills for raising Revenue shall originate in the House of Representatives; but the Senate may propose or concur with Amendments as on the other Bills.

(2) Every Bill which shall have passed the House of Representatives and the Senate, shall, before it become a Law, be presented to the President of the United States; If he approve he shall sign it, but if not he shall return it, with his Objections to that House in which it shall have originated, who shall enter the Objections at large on their Journal, and proceed to reconsider it. If after such Reconsideration two thirds of that House shall agree to pass the Bill, it shall be sent, together with the Objections, to the other House, by which it shall likewise be reconsidered, and if approved by two thirds of that House, it shall become a Law. But in all such Cases the Votes of both Houses shall be determined by Yeas and Nays, and the Names of the Persons voting for and against the Bill shall he entered on the Journal of each House respectively. If any Bill shall not be returned by the President within ten Days (Sundays excepted) after it shall have been presented to him, the Same shall be a Law, in like Manner as if he had signed it, unless the Congress by their Adjournment prevent its Return, in which Case it shall not be Law.

(3) Every Order, Resolution, or Vote to which the Concurrence of the Senate and House of Representatives may be necessary (except on a question of Adjournment) shall be presented to the President of the United States; and before the Same shall take Effect, shall be approved by him, or being disapproved by him, shall be repassed by two thirds of the Senate and House of Representatives, according to the Rules and Limitations prescribed in the Case of a Bill.

## Section 8

(1) The Congress shall have Power To lay and collect Taxes, Duties, Imposts and Excises, to pay the Debts and provide for the common Defence and general Welfare of the United States; but all Duties, Imposts and Excises shall be uniform throughout the United States;

(2) To borrow Money on the Credit of the United States;

(3) To regulate Commerce with foreign Nations, and among the several States, and with the Indian Tribes;

(4) To establish an uniform Rule of Naturalization, and uniform Laws on the subject of Bankruptcies throughout the United States;

(5) To coin Money, regulate the Value thereof, and of foreign Coin, and fix the Standard of Weights and Measures;

(6) To provide for the Punishment of counterfeiting the Securities and current Coin of the United States;

(7) To establish Post Offices and post Roads;

(8) To promote the Progress of Science and useful Arts, by securing for limited Times to Authors and Inventors the exclusive Right to their respective Writings and Discoveries;

(9) To constitute Tribunals inferior to the supreme Court;

(10) To define and punish Piracies and Felonies committed on the high Seas, and Offences against the Law of Nations;

(11) To declare War, grant Letters of Marque and Reprisal, and make Rules concerning Captures on Land and Water;

(12) To raise and support Armies, but no Appropriation of Money to that Use shall be for a longer Term than two Years;

(13) To provide and maintain a Navy;

(14) To make rules for the Government and Regulation of the land and naval Forces;

(15) To provide for calling forth the Militia to execute the Laws of the Union, suppress Insurrections and repel Invasions;

(16) To provide for organizing, arming, and disciplining, the Militia, and for governing such Part of them as may be employed in the Service of the United States, reserving to the States respectively, the Appointment of the Officers, and the Authority of training the Militia according to the discipline prescribed by Congress;

(17) To exercise exclusive Legislation in all Cases whatsoever, over such District (not exceeding ten Miles square), as may, by Cession of particular States, and the Acceptance of Congress, become the Seat of the Government of the United States, and to exercise like Authority over all Places purchased by the consent of the Legislature of the State in which the Same shall be for the Erection of Forts, Magazines, Arsenals, dock-Yards, and other needful Buildings; – And

(18) To make all Laws which shall be necessary and proper for carrying into Execution the foregoing Powers, and all other Powers vested by this Constitution in the Government of the United States, or in any Department or Officer thereof.

## Section 9

(1) The Migration or Importation of such Persons as any of the States now existing shall think proper to admit, shall not be prohibited by the Congress prior to the Year one thousand eight hundred and eight, but a Tax or duty may be imposed on such Importation, not exceeding ten dollars for each Person.

(2) The Privilege of the Writ of Habeas Corpus shall not be suspended, unless when in Cases of Rebellion or Invasion the public Safety may require it.

(3) No Bill of Attainder or ex post facto Law shall be passed.

(4) No Capitation, or other direct, Tax shall be laid, unless in Proportion to the Census or Enumeration herein before directed to be taken.

(5) No Tax or Duty shall be laid on Articles exported from any State.

(6) No preference shall be given by any Regulation of Commerce or Revenue to the Ports of one State over those of another: nor shall Vessels bound to, or from, one State, be obliged to enter, clear, or pay Duties in another.

(7) No Money shall be drawn from the Treasury, but in Consequence of Appropriations made by Law; and a regular Statement and Account of the Receipts and Expenditures of all public Money shall be published from time to time.

(8) No Title of Nobility shall be granted by the United States: And no Person holding any Office of Profit or Trust under them, shall, without the Consent of the Congress, accept of any present, Emolument, Office, or Title, of any kind whatever, from any King, Prince, or foreign State.

## Section 10

(1) No State shall enter into any Treaty, Alliance, or Confederation; grant Letters of Marque and Reprisal; coin Money; emit Bills of Credit; make any Thing but gold and silver Coin a Tender in Payment of Debts; pass any Bill of Attainder, ex post facto Law, or Law impairing the Obligation of Contracts, or grant any Title of Nobility.

(2) No State shall, without the Consent of the Congress, lay any Imposts or Duties on Imports or Exports, except what may be absolutely necessary for executing its inspection Laws: and the net Produce of all Duties and Imposts, laid by any State on Imports or Exports, shall be for the Use of the Treasury of the United States; and all such Laws shall be subject to the Revision and Controul of the Congress.

(3) No State shall, without the Consent of Congress, lay any Duty of Tonnage, keep Troops, or Ships of War in time of Peace, enter into any Agreement or Compact with another State, or with a foreign Power, or engage in War, unless actually invaded or in such imminent Danger as will not admit of delay.

## Article II
### Section 1

(1) The executive Power shall be vested in a President of the United States of America. He shall hold his Office during the Term of four Years, and, together with the Vice President, chosen for the same term, be elected, as follows:

(2) Each State shall appoint, in such Manner as the Legislature thereof may direct, a Number of Electors, equal to the whole Number of Senators and Representatives to which the State may be entitled in the Congress: but no Senator or Representative, or Person holding an Office of Trust or Profit under the United States, shall be appointed an Elector.

(3) The Electors shall meet in their respective States, and vote by Ballot for two Persons, of whom one at least shall not be an Inhabitant of the same State with themselves. And they shall make a List of all the Persons voted for, and of the Number of Votes for each; which List they shall sign and certify, and transmit sealed to the Seat of the Government of the United States, directed to the President of the Senate. The President of the Senate shall, in the Presence of the Senate and House of Representatives, open all the Certificates, and the Votes shall then be counted. The Person having the greatest Number of Votes shall be the President, if such number be a Majority of the whole Number of Electors appointed; and if there be more than one who have such Majority, and have an equal Number of Votes, then the House of Representatives shall immediately chuse by Ballot one of them for President: and if no Person have a Majority, then from the five highest on the List the said House shall in like manner chuse the President. But in chusing the President, the Votes shall be taken by States, the Representation from each State having one Vote; A quorum for this Purpose shall consist of a Member or Members from two thirds of the States, and a majority of all the States shall be necessary to a Choice. In every Case, after the Choice of the President, the Person having the greatest Number of Votes of the Electors shall be the Vice President. But if there should remain two or more who have equal Votes, the Senate shall chuse from them by Ballot the Vice President.

(4) The Congress may determine the Time of chusing the Electors, and the Day on which they shall give their Votes; which Day shall be the same throughout the United States.

(5) No Person except a natural born Citizen, or a Citizen of the United States, at the time of the Adoption of this Constitution, shall be eligible to the Office of President; neither shall any Person be eligible to that Office who shall not have attained to the Age of thirty-five Years, and been fourteen Years a Resident within

the United States.

(6) In Case of the Removal of the President from Office, or of his Death, Resignation, or Inability to discharge the Powers and Duties of the said Office, the Same shall devolve on the Vice President, and the Congress may by Law provide for the Case of Removal, Death, Resignation or Inability, both of the President and Vice President, declaring what Officer shall then act as President, and such Officer shall act accordingly, until the Disability be removed, or a President shall be elected.

(7) The President shall, at stated Times, receive for his Services, a Compensation, which shall neither be encreased nor diminished during the Period for which he shall have been elected, and he shall not receive within that Period any other Emolument from the United States, or any of them.

(8) Before he enter on the Execution of his Office, he shall take the following Oath or Affirmation: – "I do solemnly swear (or affirm) that I will faithfully execute the Office of President of the United States, and will to the best of my Ability, preserve, protect and defend the Constitution of the United States."

## Section 2

(1) The President shall be Commander in Chief of the Army and Navy of the United States, and of the Militia of the several States, when called into the actual Service of the United States; he may require the Opinion, in writing, of the principal Officer in each of the executive Departments, upon any Subject relating to the Duties of their respective Offices, and he shall have Power to grant Reprieves and Pardons for Offences against the United States, except in Cases of Impeachment.

(2) He shall have Power, by and with the Advice and Consent of the Senate, to make Treaties, provided two thirds of the Senators present concur; and he shall nominate, and by and with the Advice and Consent of the Senate, shall appoint Ambassadors, other public Ministers and Consuls, Judges of the supreme Court, and all other Officers of the United States, whose Appointments are not herein otherwise provided for, and which shall be established by Law: but the Congress may by Law vest the Appointment of such inferior Officers, as they think proper, in the President alone, in the Courts of Law, or in the Heads of Departments.

(3) The President shall have Power to fill up all Vacancies that may happen during the Recess of the Senate, by granting Commissions which shall expire at the End of their next Session.

## Section 3

He shall from time to time give to the Congress Information of the State of the Union, and recommend to their Consideration such Measures as he shall judge necessary and expedient; he may, on extraordinary Occasions, convene both Houses, or either of them, and in Case of Disagreement between them, with Respect to the Time of Adjournment, he may adjourn them to such Time as he shall think proper; he shall receive Ambassadors and other public Ministers; he shall take Care that the Laws be faithfully executed, and shall Commission all the Officers of the United States.

## Section 4

The President, Vice President and all civil Officers of the United States, shall be removed from Office on Impeachment for, and Conviction of, Treason, Bribery, orother High Crimes and Misdemeanors.

## Article III

### Section 1

The judicial Power of the United States, shall be vested in one supreme Court, and in such inferior Courts as the Congress may from time to time ordain and establish. The Judges, both of the supreme and inferior Courts, shall hold theirOffices during good Behaviour, and shall, at stated Times, receive for their Services, a Compensation, which shall not be diminished during their Continuance in Office.

### Section 2

(1) The judicial Power shall extend to all Cases, in Law and Equity, arising under this Constitution, the Laws of the United States, and Treaties made, or which shall be made, under their Authority; – to all Cases affecting Ambassadors, other public Ministers and Consuls; – to all cases of admiralty and maritime Jurisdiction; – to Controversies between two or more States; between a State and Citizens of another State; – between Citizens of different States; – between Citizens of the same State claiming Lands under Grants of different States, and between a State, or the Citizens thereof, and foreign States, Citizens or Subjects.

(2) In all Cases affecting Ambassadors, other public Ministers and Consuls, and those in which a State shall be Party, the supreme Court shall have original Jurisdiction. In all the other Cases before mentioned, the supreme Court shall have appellate Jurisdiction, both as to Law and Fact, with such Exceptions, and under such Regulations as the Congress shall make.

(3) The Trial of all Crimes, except in Cases of Impeachment, shall be by jury; and such Trial shall be held in the State where the said Crimes shall have been committed; but when not committed within any State, the Trial shall be at such Place or Places as the Congress may by Law have directed.

### Section 3

(1) Treason against the United States, shall consist only in levying War against them, or in adhering to their Enemies, giving them Aid and Comfort. No Persons shall be convicted of Treason unless on the Testimony of two Witnesses to the same overt Act, or on Confession in open Court.

(2) The Congress shall have Power to declare the Punishment of Treason, but no Attainder of Treason shall work Corruption of Blood, or Forfeiture except during the Life of the Person attainted.

## Article IV

### Section 1

Full Faith and Credit shall be given in each State to the public Acts, Records, and judicial Proceedings of every other State. And the Congress may by general Laws prescribe the Manner in which such Acts, Records and Proceedings shall be proved, and the Effect therof.

### Section 2

(1) The Citizens of each State shall be entitled to all Privileges and Immunities of Citizens in the several States.

(2) A Person charged in any State with Treason, Felony, or other Crime, who shall flee from Justice, and be found in another State, shall on Demand of the executive

Authority of the State from which he fled, be delivered up, to be removed to the State having Jurisdiction of the Crime.

(3) No person held to Service or Labour in one State, under the Laws thereof, escaping into another, shall, in Consequence of any Law or Regulation therein, be discharged from such Service or Labour, but shall be delivered up on Claim of the Party to whom such Service or Labour may be due.

## Section 3

(1) New States may be admitted by the Congress into this Union; but no new State shall be formed or erected within the Jurisdiction of any other State; nor any State be formed by the Junction of two or more States, or Parts of States, without the Consent of the Legislatures of the States concerned as well as of the Congress.

(2) The Congress shall have Power to dispose of and make all needful Rules and Regulations respecting the Territory or other Property belonging to the United States; and nothing in this Constitution shall be so construed as to Prejudice any Claims of the United States, or of any particular State.

## Section 4

The United States shall guarantee to every State in this Union a Republican Form of Government, and shall protect each of them against Invasion; and on Application of the Legislature, or of the Executive (when the Legislature cannot be convened) against domestic Violence.

## Article V

The Congress, whenever two thirds of both Houses shall deem it necessary, shall propose Amendments to this Constitution, or, on the Application of the Legislatures of two. thirds of the several States, shall call a Convention for proposing Amendments, which, in either Case, shall be valid to all Intents and Purposes, as Part of this Constitution, when ratified by the Legislatures of three fourths of the several States, or by Conventions in three fourths thereof, as the one or the other Mode of Ratification may be proposed by the Congress; Provided that no Amendment which may be made prior to the Year One thousand eight hundred and eight shall in any Manner affect the first and fourth Clauses in the Ninth Section of the first Article; and that no State, without its Consent, shall be deprived of its equal Suffrage in the Senate.

## Article VI

(1) All Debts contracted and Engagements entered into, before the Adoption of this Constitution, shall be as valid against the United States under this Constitution, as under the Confederation.

(2) This Constitution, and the Laws of the United States which shall be made in Pursuance thereof; and all Treaties made, or which shall be made, under the Authority of the United States, shall be the supreme Law of the Land; and the Judges in every State shall be bound thereby, any Thing in the Constitution or Laws of any State to the Contrary notwithstanding.

(3) The Senators and Representatives before mentioned, and the Members of the several State Legislatures, and all executive and judicial Officers, both of the United States and of the several States, shall be bound by Oath or Affirmation, to support this Constitution; but no religious Test shall ever be required as a Qualification to any Office or public Trust under the United States.

## Article VII

The Ratification of the Conventions of nine States, shall be sufficient for the Establishment of this Constitution between the states so ratifying the Same. Done in Convention by the Unanimous Consent of the States present the Seventeenth Day of September in the Year of our Lord one thousand seven hundred and Eighty seven and of the Independence of the United States of America the Twelfth, In witness whereof We have hereunto subscribed our Names.

# Articles In Addition To, And Amendment Of, The Constitution.

(The first 10 Amendments were ratified December 15, 1791,
and form what is known as the "Bill of Rights")

## Amendment I

Congress shall make no law respecting an establishment of religion, or prohibiting the free exercise thereof; or abridging the freedom of speech, or of the press; or the right of the people peaceably to assemble, and to petition the Government for a redress of grievances.

## Amendment II

A well regulated Militia, being necessary to the security of a free State, the right of the people to keep and bear Arms, shall not be infringed.

## Amendment III

No Soldier shall, in time of peace be quartered in any house, without the consent of the Owner, nor in time of war, but in a manner to be prescribed by law.

## Amendment IV

The right of the people to be secure in their persons, houses, papers, and effects, against unreasonable searches and seizures, shall not be violated, and no Warrants shall issue, but upon probable cause, supported by Oath or affirmation, and particularly describing the place to be searched, and the persons or things to be seized.

## Amendment V

No person shall be held to answer for a capital, or otherwise infamous crime, unless on a presentment or indictment of a Grand jury, except in cases arising in the land or naval forces, or in the Militia, when in actual service in time of War or public danger; nor shall any person be subject for the same offence to be twice put in jeopardy of life or limb; nor shall be compelled in any criminal case to be a witness against himself, nor be deprived of life, liberty, or property, without due process of law; nor shall private property be taken for public use, without just compensation.

## Amendment VI

In all criminal prosecutions, the accused shall enjoy the right to a speedy and public trial, by an impartial jury of the State and district wherein the crime shall have been committed, which district shall have been previously ascertained by law, and to be informed of the nature and cause of the accusation; to be confronted with the witnesses against him; to have compulsory process for obtaining witnesses in his favor, and to have the Assistance of Counsel for his defence.

## Amendment VII

In Suits at common law, where the value in controversy shall exceed twenty dollars, the right of trial by jury shall be preserved, and no fact tried by a jury, shall be otherwise reexamined in any Court of the United States, than according to the rules of the common law.

## Amendment VIII

Excessive bail shall not be required, nor excessive fines imposed, nor cruel and unusual punishment inflicted.

## Amendment IX

The enumeration in the Constitution, of certain rights, shall not be construed to deny or disparage others retained by the people.

## Amendment X

The powers not delegated to the United States by the Constitution, nor prohibited by it to the States, are reserved to the States respectively, or to the people.

## Amendment XI

*(Ratified February 7, 1795)*

The judicial power of the United States shall not be construed to extend to any suit in law or equity, commenced or prosecuted against one of the United States by Citizens of another State, or by Citizens or Subjects of any Foreign State.

## Amendment XII

*(Ratified July 27, 1804)*

The Electors shall meet in their respective states and vote by ballot for President and Vice-President, one of whom, at least, shall not be an inhabitant of the same state with themselves; they shall name in their ballots the person voted for as President, and in distinct ballots the person voted for as Vice-President, and they shall make distinct lists of all persons voted for as President, and of all persons voted for as VicePresident, and of the number of votes for each, which lists they shall sign and certify, and transmit sealed to the seat of the government of the United States, directed to the President of the Senate; – The person having the greatest number of votes for President, shall be the President, if such number be a majority of the whole number of Electors appointed; and if no person have such majority, then from the persons having the highest numbers not exceeding three on the list of those voted for as President, the House of Representatives shall choose immediately, by ballot, the President. But in choosing the President, the votes shall be taken by states, the representation from each state having one vote; a quorum for this purpose shall consist of a member or members from two-thirds of the states, and a majority of all the states shall be necessary to a choice. And if the House of Representatives shall not choose a President whenever the right of choice shall devolve upon them, before the fourth day of March next following, then the Vice-President shall act as President, as in the case of the death or other constitutional disability of the President. – The person having the greatest number of votes as Vice-President, shall be the Vice-President, if such number be a majority of the whole number of Electors appointed, and if no person have a majority, then from the two highest numbers on the list, the Senate shall choose the Vice-President; a quorum for the purpose shall consist of two-thirds of the whole number of Senators, and a majority of the whole number shall be necessary to a choice. But no person constitutionally ineligible to the office of President shall be eligible to that of Vice-President of the United States.

## Amendment XIII
*(Ratified December 6, 1865)*

### Section 1
Neither slavery nor involuntary servitude, except as a punishment for crime whereof the party shall have been duly convicted, shall exist within the United States, or any place subject to their jurisdiction.

### Section 2
Congress shall have power to enforce this article by appropriate legislation.

## Amendment XIV
*(Ratified July 9, 1868)*

### Section 1
All persons born or naturalized in the United States, and subject to the jurisdiction thereof, are citizens of the United States and of the State wherein they reside. No State shall make or enforce any law which shall abridge the privileges or immunities of citizens of the United States; nor shall any State deprive any person of life, liberty, or property, without due process of law; nor deny to any person within its jurisdiction the equal protection of the laws.

### Section 2
Representatives shall be apportioned among the several States according to their respective numbers, counting the whole number of persons in each State, excluding Indians not taxed. But when the right to vote at any election for the choice of electors for President and Vice President of the United States, Representatives in Congress, the Executive and Judicial officers of a State, or the members of the Legislature thereof, is denied to any of the male inhabitants of such State, being twenty-one years of age, and citizens of the United States, or in any way abridged, except for participation in rebellion, or other crime, the basis of representation therein shall be reduced in the proportion which the number of such male citizens shall bear to the whole number of male citizens twenty-one years of age in such State.

### Section 3
No person shall be a Senator or Representative in Congress, or elector of President and Vice President, or hold any office, civil or military, under the United States, or under any State, who, having previously taken an oath, as a member of Congress, or as an officer of the United States, or as a member of any State legislature, or as an executive or judicial officer of any State, to support the Constitution of the United States, shall have engaged in insurrection or rebellion against the same, or given aid

or comfort to the enemies thereof. But Congress may by a vote of two-thirds of each House, remove such disability.

## Section 4

The validity of the public debt of the United States, authorized by law, including debts incurred for payment of pensions and bounties for services in suppressing insurrection or rebellion, shall not be questioned. But neither the United States nor any State shall assume or pay any debt or obligation incurred in aid of insurrection or rebellion against the United States, or any claim for the loss or emancipation of any slave; but all such debts, obligations and claims shall be held illegal and void.

## Section 5

The Congress shall have power to enforce, by appropriate legislation, the provisions of this article.

## Amendment XV

*(Ratified February 3, 1870)*

## Section 1

The right of citizens of the United States to vote shall not be denied or abridged by the United States or by any State on account of race, color, or previous condition of servitude.

## Section 2

The Congress shall have power to enforce this article by appropriate legislation.

## Amendment XVI

*(Ratified February 3, 1913)*

The Congress shall have power to lay and collect taxes on incomes, from whatever source derived, without apportionment among the several States, and without regard to any census or enumeration.

## Amendment XVII

*(Ratified April 8, 1915)*

(1) The Senate of the United States shall be composed of two Senators from each State, elected by the people thereof for six years; and each Senator shall have one vote. The electors in each State shall have the qualifications requisite for electors of the most numerous branch of the State legislatures.

(2) When vacancies happen in the representation of any State in the Senate, the executive authority of such State shall issue writs of election to fill such vacancies: Provided, That the legislature of any State may empower the executive thereof to make temporary appointments until the people fill the vacancies by election as the legislature may direct.

(3) This amendment shall not be so construed as to affect the election or term of any Senator chosen before it becomes valid as part of the Constitution.

## Amendment XVIII

*(Ratified January 16, 1919. Repealed December 5, 1933 by Amendment 21)*

## Section 1

After one year from the ratification of this article the manufacture, sale, or transportation of intoxicating liquors within, the importation thereof into, or the exportation thereof from the United States and all territory subject to the jurisdiction thereof for beverage purposes is hereby prohibited.

## Section 2

The Congress and the several States shall have concurrent power to enforce this article by appropriate legislation.

## Section 3

This article shall be inoperative unless it shall have been ratified as an amendment to the Constitution by the legislatures of the several States as provided in the Constitution, within seven years from the date of the submission hereof to the States by the Congress.

## Amendment XIX

*(Ratified August 18, 1920)*

(1) The right of citizens of the United States to vote shall not be denied or abridged by the United States or by any State on account of sex.

(2) Congress shall have power to enforce this article by appropriate legislation.

## Amendment XX

*(Ratified January 23, 1933)*

## Section 1

The terms of the President and Vice-President shall end at noon on the 20th day of January, and the terms of Senators and Representatives at noon on the 3d day of January, of the years in which such terms would have ended if this article had not been ratified; and the terms of their successors shall then begin.

## Section 2

The Congress shall assemble at least once in every year, and such meeting shall begin at noon on the 3d day of January, unless they shall by law appoint a different day.

## Section 3

If, at the time fixed for the beginning of the term of the President, the President elect shall have died, the Vice President elect shall become President. If a President shall not have been chosen before the time fixed for the beginning of his term, or if the President elect shall have failed to qualify, then the Vice President elect shall act as President until a President shall have qualified; and the Congress may by law provide for the case wherein neither a President elect nor a Vice President elect shall have qualified, declaring who shall then act as President, or the manner in which one who is to act shall be selected, and such person shall act accordingly until a President or Vice President shall have qualified.

## Section 4

The Congress may by law provide for the case of the death of any of the persons from whom the House of Representatives may choose a President whenever the right of choice shall have devolved upon them, and for the case of the death of any of the persons from whom the Senate may choose a Vice President whenever the right of choice shall have devolved upon them.

## Section 5

Sections 1 and 2 shall take effect on the 15th day of October following the ratification of this article.

## Section 6

This article shall be inoperative unless it shall have been ratified as an amendment to the Constitution by the legislatures of three-fourths of the several States within seven years from the date of its submission.

## Amendment XXI

*(Ratified December 5, 1933)*

## Section 1

The eighteenth article of amendment to the Constitution of the United States is hereby repealed.

## Section 2

The transportation or importation into any State, Territory, orpossession of the United States for delivery or use therein of intoxicating liquors, in violation of the laws thereof, is hereby prohibited.

## Section 3

This article shall be inoperative unless it shall have been ratified as an amendment to the Constitution by conventions in the several States, as provided in the Constitution, within seven years from the date of the submission hereof to the States by the Congress.

## Amendment XXII

*(Ratified February 27, 1951)*

## Section 1

No person shall be elected to the office of the President more than twice, and no person who has held the office of President, or acted as President, for more than two years of a term to which some other person was elected President shall be elected to the office of the President more than once. But this Article shall not apply to any person holding the office of President when this Article was proposed by the Congress, and shall not prevent any person who may be holding the office of President, or acting as President, during the term within which this Article becomes operative from holding the office of President or acting as President during the remainder of such term.

## Section 2

This article shall be inoperative unless it shall have been ratified as an amendment to the Constitution by the legislatures of three-fourths of the several States within seven years from the date of its submission to the States by the Congress.

## Amendment XXIII

*(Ratified March 29, 1961)*

## Section 1

(1) The District constituting the seat of Government of the United States shall appoint in such manner as the Congress may direct:

(2) A number of electors of President and Vice President equal to the whole number of Senators and Representatives in Congress to which the District would be entitled if it were a State, but in no event more than the least populous State; they shall be in addition to those appointed by the States, but they shall be considered, for the purposes of the election of President and Vice President, to be electors appointed by a State; and they shall meet in the District and perform such duties as provided by the twelfth article of amendment.

## Section 2

The Congress shall have power to enforce this article by appropriate legislation.

### Amendment XXIV

*(Ratified January 23, 1964)*

## Section 1

The right of citizens of the United States to vote in any primary or other election for President or Vice-President, for electors for President or Vice President, or for Senator or Representative in Congress, shall not be denied or abridged by the United States or any State by reason of failure to pay any poll tax or other tax.

## Section 2

The Congress shall have power to enforce this article by appropriate legislation.

### Amendment XXV

*(Ratified February 10, 1967)*

## Section 1

In case of the removal of the President from office or of his death or resignation, the Vice President shall become President.

## Section 2

Whenever there is a vacancy in the office of the Vice President, the President shall nominate a Vice President who shall take office upon confirmation by a majority vote of both Houses of Congress.

## Section 3

Whenever the President transmits to the President pro tempore of the Senate and Speaker of the House of Representatives his written declaration that he is unable to discharge the powers and duties of his office, and until he transmits to them a written declaration to the contrary, such powers and duties shall be discharged by the Vice President as Acting President.

## Section 4

(1) Whenever the Vice President and a majority of either the principal officers of the executive departments or of such other body as Congress may by law provide, transmit to the President pro tempore of the Senate and the Speaker of the House of Representatives their written declaration that the President is unable to discharge

the powers and duties of his office, the Vice President shall immediately assume the powers and duties of the office as Acting President.

(2) Thereafter, when the President transmits to the President pro tempore of the Senate and the Speaker of the House of Representatives has written declaration that no inability exists, he shall resume the powers and duties of his office unless the Vice President and a majority of either the principal officers of the executive department or of such other body as Congress may by law provide, transmit within four days to the President pro tempore of the Senate and the Speaker of the House of Representatives their written declaration that the President is unable to discharge the powers and duties of his office. Thereupon Congress shall decide the issue, assembling within forty-eight hours for that purpose if not in session. If the Congress, within twenty-one days after receipt of the latter written declaration, or, if Congress is not in session, within twenty-one days after Congress is required to assemble, determines by two-thirds vote of both Houses that the President is unable to discharge the powers and duties of his office, the Vice President shall continue to discharge the same as Acting President; otherwise, the President shall resume the powers and duties of his office.

## Amendment XXVI

*(Ratified July 1, 1971)*

### Section 1

The right of citizens of the United States, who are eighteen years of age or older, to vote shall not he denied or unabridged by the United States or by any State on account of age.

### Section 2

The Congress shall have the power to enforce this article by appropriate legislation.

## Amendment XXVII

*(Ratified May 7, 1992)*

No law, varying the compensation for the services of the Senators and Representatives, shall take effect, until an election of Representatives shall have intervened.

# Suggested Legislation for State Legislatures

AN ACT TO REQUIRE DURING THE HIGH SCHOOL YEARS THE TEACHING OF A FULL SEMESTER COURSE ON THE FOUNDERS' PRINCIPLES WHICH ARE THE FOUNDATION OF OUR FORM OF GOVERNMENT FOR A FREE PEOPLE AS INCORPORATED IN THE DECLARATION OF INDEPENDENCE, THE UNITED STATES CONSTITUTION, AND THE FEDERALIST PAPERS

Whereas, the adoption of the Declaration of Independence in 1776 and the signing of the United States Constitution in 1787 were seminal events in the history of the United States, the Declaration of Independence providing the philosophical foundation on which the nation rests, and the Constitution of the United States providing its structure of government; and

Whereas, the Federalist Papers embody the most eloquent and forceful argument made in support of the adoption of our republican form of government; and

Whereas, these documents, along with the writings of the Founders, stand as the foundation of our form of democracy, providing at the same time the touchstone of our national identity and the vehicle for orderly growth and change; and

Whereas, these Founding Documents established a set of principles, known as the FOUNDERS' PRINCIPLES, which are the heart and soul of a government for a free society; and

Whereas, these principles enabled a group of 13 colonies to become the greatest and most powerful nation on earth in a relatively short period of time; and

Whereas, most Americans do not know about nor understand the timely and timeless importance of these principles to our form of government and to their current lives; and

Whereas, the survival of the republic requires that our nation's children, the future guardians of its heritage and participants in its governance, have a clear understanding of these principles and the importance of their preservation; now therefore,

The General Assembly of North Carolina enacts:

Section 1. G. S. 115C-81 is amended by adding a new subsection to read:

(q) Civic Literacy:

(1) Local boards of education shall require during the high school years the teaching of a full semester course on

a) the philosophical foundations of our form of government

b) the principles underlying the Declaration of Independence, the United States Constitution, and the Federalist Papers, which are the principles of government for a free people and are known as the Founders' Principles.

(2) Local boards of education shall include among the requirements for graduation from high school a passing grade in a full semester course on the principles underlying the Declaration of Independence, the United States Constitution, and the Federalist Papers.

(3) The State Board of Education shall require that any curriculum-based tests administered statewide beginning with 2011-2012 academic year include questions related to the principles underlying the Declaration of Independence, the United States Constitution, and the most important arguments of the Federalist Papers.

(4) The State Department of Public Instruction and the local boards of education, as appropriate, shall provide curriculum content for the semester course and teacher training to ensure that the intent and provisions of this subsection are carried out.

(5) The Department of Public Instruction shall submit a biennial report to the General Assembly covering:

a) The implementation of this subsection; and

b) The statewide student results from the State curriculum-based tests administered in accordance with subdivision 3 of this subsection.

Section 2 This act is effective when it becomes law and applies beginning with the 2011-2012 school year.

# Sources

## Chapter 1

1. Jefferson, Thomas. Thomas Jefferson's annotated copy of the Federalist Papers. (http://www.loc.gov/exhibits/jefferson/jefffed.html)

2. wiseGEEK. "What Was the Population of the U. S. Throughout Its History?" (http://www.wisegeek.com/what-was-the-population-of-the-us-throughout Its-history.htm) (8/30/2009).

3. Rosseau, Jean Jacques.)"The Social Contract."

## Chapter 2

4. Jefferson, Thomas. "Resolutions Relative to the Alien and Sedition Acts." Nov, 10, 1798. Writings 17:379—80,385—91. (http://press-pubs.uchicago.edu/founders/documents/vlch8s41.html)

## Chapter 3

5. North Carolina Magazine. June 1979. p. 12.

6. U. S. Department of State., "Growth of Government Intervention in the Economy."

7. Will, George Column."A Doctrine of No Retreat." Townhall.com.(8/23/2009). Quoting Senator Lamar Alexander (R) TN.

8. Madison, James. "Federalist 62." (http://whycongresscantread.com/research/madisonjames/bewarelaws)

## Chapter 4

9. Jackson, President Andrew."Farewell Address." March 4, 1837.

10. Paul, Congressman Ron. "House Bill H.R.1207 and Senate Bill S. 604." 2009 session of the U.S. Congress.

11. Jefferson, Thomas. "Thomas Jefferson to John Taylor." 1816. ME 15:23 (http://etext.virginia.edu/jefferson/quotations/jeff1340.htm)

12. Madison, James. "Letter to Henry Lee." 1790. (http://www.lexrex.com/enlightened/Americanideal/yardstick/pr11-quotes).

13. Jefferson, Thomas. "Thomas Jefferson to Samuel Kercheval." Monticello. July 12, 1816. (http://quotes.libertytree.ca/quote_blog/Thomas.Jefferson.Quote.0564)

14. Dailey Reckoning. "Fiat Currency: Using the Past to See Into the Future." (http://daileyreckoning.com/fiat-currency) (10/23/2009).

15. Ibid.

16. Jackson, Andrew. "Farewell Address." March 4, 1837

17. Kelo v. City of New London. 545 U.S. 469 (2005)

18. Adams, John. " A Defence of the Constitutions of Government of the United States…" March 22, 1778.

19. O'Connor, Sandra Day. "Federalism". The Trashing of America: Assault on the Tenth Amendment. http://www.jeremiahproject.com/trashingamerica/10thamendment.html)

20. Hamilton, Alexander. "Federalist 78."

21. Jefferson, Thomas. "Letter to William C. Jarvis." September 28, 1820. (http:///www.monticello.org/reports/quotes/education.html)

22. Washington, President George. "Farewell Address." 1796. Wickipedia: Address originally published in David Claypoole's American Dailey Advertiser on September 19, 1796. P. 198.

23. Northwest Ordinance of 1787, "An Ordinance For The Government Of The Territory Of The United States Northwest Of The Ohio River". *Our Ageless Constitution. P. 192.*

24. Washington, President George. "Farewell Address" (1796), Ibid., p. 198.

25. Jefferson, President Thomas. "First Inaugural Address." Ibid. p 206.

26. Eagle Forum, "North American Union? Connecting the Dots." 2008.

27. Peterson, Daneen G., PhD. "About the NAU—What You Don't Know Can Hurt You." Speech in Washington, D. C. June 15, 2007.

28. New, David D. (with Cliff Kincaid), "Michael New—Mercenary...or American Soldier."

29. Madison, James. "The Writings of James Madison."
Vol 6 (correspondemce 1790-1802)-Charters. 2-Para.186.

30. Thompson, Nicholas. "Waging War Over the Constitution and Its Framers."
Los Angeles Times, 8/14/2005.

31. Center for Individual Freedom, UN Monitor, "Global Taxes Are Back, Watch Your Wallet," 12/30/2009.
(http://www.cfif.org/htdocs/freedomline/un_monitor/in_our_opin ion/global_taxes.htm).

32. Phyllis Schlafly Report, "Obama's New World Order", March, 2009.

33. Drucker, Peter F. "Post-Capitalist Society," p.150.

34. Book Rags, "War Powers Act/ Americans at War: 1946-2005 Summary,"
(http://www.bookrags.com/research/war-powers-act-aaw-04/).

35. Story, Justice Joseph. 0 "Commentaries on the Constitution", 2nd edition volume 2, Chapter 45, p. 617 (1851).

# THE DESTRUCTION OF
## *The* GREAT AMERICAN DREAM

---

## ORDER FORM

---

To order more copies of
*The Destruction of the Great American Dream*
use the order form below for payment by **check or money order only**

---

*Please send the following copies of "The Destruction of the Great American Dream":*

Qty._____copies at $9.95 per copy.　　　Name_____

Book Total:_____　　　Address_____

NC Residents Add 7.75% Sales Tax:_____　　City_____

Total Amount Enclosed:_____　　State_____Zip_____

**mail to: Sedgefield Graphics**
**5313 High Point Road**
**Greensboro, NC 27407**

---

## To order by *credit card*
### VISIT OUR WEBSITE
### FOUNDERSPRINCIPLES.COM

*Our Ageless Constitution*

# ORDER FORM

*Edited by*
**W. David Stedman**
**LaVaughn G. Lewis**

*The celebration and rediscovery of a unique and enduring document...a book for all Americans ...a keepsake for all times!*

*Our Ageless Constitution is a comprehensive sourcebook that:*

• *Presents the basic principles of the Constitution in 25 concise. one page essays.*

• *Traces the roots of the Constitution in the Roman, Greek and British philosophy and experience.*

• *Raises an alarm over the erosion of certain Constitutionally guaranteed liberties.*

• *Documents the role of religion in the founding of the nation and puts in the proper perspective.*

• *Encourages all Americans, especially our students, to rediscover the essence of American's greatness by understanding the Founder's Principles.*

*Our Ageless Constitution spans 320 pages and is quality bound. Fully illustrated, painstakingly researched and extensively indexed, it is as much at home on the coffee table as the library shelf.*

*To order Our Ageless Constitution by* **check or money order only** *use the order form below*

---

*Please send the following copies of "Our Ageless Constitution":*

*Qty.\_\_\_\_copies at $29.95 per copy.*

*Book Total:_____*

*NC Residents Add 7.75% Sales Tax:_____*

*Total Amount Enclosed:_____*

*Name_____*

*Address_____*

*City_____*

*State_____Zip_____*

**mail to: Sedgefield Graphics**
**5313 High Point Road**
**Greensboro, NC 27407**

---

TO ORDER BY CREDIT CARD VISIT OUR WEBSITE: **OURAGELESSCONSTITUTION.COM**

NOTES

NOTES

# NOTES

NOTES